TALKING ZAPPA

With

Tony Trombo

Copyright (c) 2024 by Tony Trombo

All rights reserved.

TALKING ZAPPA with Tony Trombo

AI transcribed from the *Mind Bender Entertainment* podcast of the same name. All show were recorded in 2014.

Summary: Tony Trombo interviews various band members from the Frank Zappa group.

1st edition

www.TonyTrombo.World

PAGES and CHAPTERS

6	Ike Willis
17	Ed Mann
29	Mike Keneally
40	Lisa Popeil
52	Howard Kaylan
65	Don Preston
80	Bobby Martin
93	Arthur Barrow
106	Cal Schenkel
117	Candy Zappa
127	Essra Mohawk

And hey everybody, it's Tony Trombo once again!

Yep... it's my new book! Believe me, I shopped it around to a few places. "It's the AI transcription of several of my Podcasts." I said. "WHY would anyone want to read IN A BOOK, what you already put out in a Podcast?" would be their question!

For a while, I actually believed that theory. Then, after listening to several of my old podcasts, I realized that I would really LIKE to be able to get to all this fun information, WITHOUT having to go through hour after hour of of intros, outros, commercials Etc. So I self published!

But problems arose...

The first thing that I encountered was that fact that I don't type very fast! Listening to a mp3 and then trying to type it out. became more than I could handle!

I tried a few services on the internet that let me to upload my content, and let their automated transcription service do all the hard work! Unfortunately, most them them (prior to decent AI service) would just type EVERYTHING in one long paragraph!

It couldn't identify one person from another, so what I got back was pretty much worthless, because I had to spend HOURS going over the whole mess, line by line, trying to figure out who is who, and formatting the paragraphs into something remotely readable!

At last I stumbled across a web service that actually used a good AI program to quickly and efficiently LISTEN to my shows, and type out a relatively good (but not perfect) transcription of my interviews!

I still had to do a BIT of editing to get it to an acceptable state, that I could feel good about releasing it to the general public.

I'll bet you're going to find a few mistakes here and there, and I'll probably have to do a few reissues to work out all the spelling / grammar bugs! I'm no editor, and I can only do SO much, and spellchecker is good, but not flawless!

So with that said, I present to you a book of interesting (at least to me) interviews with people that I have been listening to for decades! The people of the Frank Zappa band!

Oh yea, I hear you asking... just HOW did I get to talk to these fantastic musicians anyway? The answer is simply Facebook! Yep, you can find just about ANYONE there, and with a quick little message, asking if they would like to give me about 30 minutes of their time to talk about their days with FZ!

Surprisingly, I only had a few people that I contacted that didn't want to do it! So I lost out. They lost out. YOU lost out! Oh well... I DID get a nice assortment of people to give me a HUGE amount of inside Zappa info!

I think that once you actually GET to play in the band with Frank, you're ALWAYS a band member! You're in a pretty exclusive club of alumni, and talking about it never gets old!

For that, I'm thankful! I'm also thankful that not ONLY did I get to talk to these people, but I've become pretty good friends with a number of them! That's just an extra bonus for me!

Thanks for your support!

Tony Trombo

IKE WILLIS

Ike Willis is an American musician best known for his work with Frank Zappa. He is a guitarist and vocalist who joined Zappa's band in the late 1970s and performed with him until Zappa's death in 1993. Willis' distinctive vocal style and energetic stage presence made him a memorable part of Zappa's live performances and recordings during that time. After Zappa's passing, Willis continued to perform and record music, sometimes collaborating with other former members of Zappa's band.

Ike Willis: Hey, Tony. How are you doing, buddy?

Tony: Hey, pretty good. I know it's Ike, but ya know, you'll be Joe to me forever!

Ike Willis: Thank you very much.

Tony: Joe's Garage. That was your first recording with Frank, wasn't it?

Ike Willis: Yes, it was. From June until August of 1979. Yes, I was 20, 21 years old. That was my first album with Frank. I'm pretty biased because that was like the incredible band and incredible tours leading up to the recording of Joe's Garage. I really had a great time doing that album. I learned so much. I learned how to produce. I learned how to engineer. I learned how to do my own albums, in fact I learned so much from him every time I walked into the door. That was always a great thing to do. Yes, that was my first. It definitely wasn't my last, that's for sure.

Tony: A lot of the guys that I talk to record with Frank for a bit, and then they actually get into the band later. It sounds like you were in the band before recording.

Ike Willis: Yes, well, he hired me in June of '78, actually, right out of college. I met him at the beginning of the *Shake Your Booty* Tour in 1977. My wife and I were students at Washington University in St. Louis. It was at the beginning of my senior year that Frank came to my campus and did an outdoor concert. I got myself on the local crew just schlepping equipment and things like that. Essentially, I was there to take notes because I always had mad respect for Frank as a composer, a producer, a businessman in the industry.

The thing was, I always had mad respect for Frank. I wasn't a Frank Zappa fan, but I'd been listening to him since I was 10 years old. First, my best friend came running over to my house when I was 10 years old in 1965 with a copy of *Freak Out*. I had no idea who Frank Zappa was and whatever. 10 years later, I ended up being in his band. It was a really bizarre thing. I'd been playing, I started playing guitar when I was 8 years old and started my first bands when I was 9 years old and back in the 60s and playing festivals and love-ins and concerts and things like that since I was 9.

When I met Frank, basically I wanted to take notes just because he was that guy. I always had so much respect for his abilities and the fact that he was so prolific at writing songs and recording and releasing albums and things like that.

By the time I met him, I'd been playing professionally for 12 years. Still, that was just scratching the surface. He was the most intelligent human being I'd ever met, the most incredible guy I'd ever met. We just hit it off right off the bat.

Tony: Now, did he hear you sing at a club or did you do it while he was there? How did he first hear you?

Ike Willis: No, I did it while he was there. I spent the whole day helping set up the equipment, schlepping equipment. I met the crew and I met everybody like that. They came in for soundcheck. We made eye contact for some reason or another. Then after soundcheck and everybody was eating and they had the hospitality room and he called me over to his table and just started talking to me. He started asking me questions. We were talking. We ended up talking for like over an hour. Then his manager came in and said it's time for him to get ready for the show. He took me into his dressing room.

He asked me if I was a musician. He asked me if I played because I stuck out like a sore thumb, I told him, well, yes, I was a guitar player and I play a little bit and I sing a little bit. He took me into his dressing room and just handed me his guitar and said, well, do any of my stuff? I said, yes, I know a few tunes. He hands me his guitar and he said, well, okay, play me something. I started playing Carolina Hardcore Ecstasy. We just started playing and singing. The rest of the guys in the band, Tommy Mars, Ed Mann, Adrian Belew, Terry Bozio, Patrick O'Hearn, walked in and everybody started singing. It was like one big hootenanny. It was actually pretty fantastic.

Of course, I was only 19 years old at the time. I was essentially thinking to myself, well, this isn't really happening and I'm dreaming, so I might as well just play along. Yes. It was actually pretty fantastic. As a result of that, he told me in our conversation, which by this time had gone past two hours, and which was making him late to start the concert, that he was looking for a lead vocalist and a front man because he really hadn't had a legitimate official front man for a few years because at that time Bozio and Adrian Belew were doing a lot of the lead vocal stuff and mostly Frank. Frank was of the opinion that he didn't want to do a lot of the lead vocals anymore. He wanted a legitimate front man and things like that. That's what he was telling me.

He asked me for my address and my phone number. After making me play and sing for him, he apparently liked what he heard. I, once again, thought this is not really happening and I'm dreaming. I'm just enjoying myself and having a great time. Plus the fact that I was really getting on the fact that Frank was so well-versed in just about everything.

I was a political science law major, actually, in college. We were speaking on science and physics and current events and things. He was well-versed in all of them. We basically hit it off right off the bat. We spent more time laughing and discussing just the current events of the world and life in America that he said, "Well, look, I've got to do this show. Give me your vital statistics. Give me your address. Give me your phone number. Because I hold auditions after every tour, when I get back to L.A., after the tour is over, and I'd like to fly you out to audition for the band." I did. He did. Eight months later, he calls me back after the *Shake Your Booty* tour was over and said "Okay, I'm back. I'm a man of my word. I will fly you out at the end of the week once I find a soundstage to set up all the equipment in. I'll fly you out to audition for the band."

I ended up making it. Actually, Arthur Barrow, he was our bass player. I also auditioned Artie. Vinnie Colaiuta was our drummer. They became the rhythm section. We all got hired on the same day, at the end of the week that I flew in. That was June of 1978. That began my adventure slash employment slash whole thing with Frank.

Tony: Now, that was a life changer. really, because you do a lot with Project Object and, Ugly Radio Rebellion, all these different groups that are doing Frank's music. It's like your whole life changed at that point.

Ike Willis: Indeed. it was a total game changer and life changer because of the fact that, like I said, at the time that we had met and then he hired me and then I was in his band and doing the albums. At that point, by the time that he passed away, I had spent basically half my life with him. Sure. because of my age, how old I was when I started playing with him. I'd been with him for over half my life.

That has always been a really important and a very important thing for me and a huge honor for me because, I didn't look at it as being, well, Frank's front man because he said, "Okay, I'm hiring you." He actually told me, "You are going to be the front man, okay? I don't want to be the lead vocalist anymore. I want you to work the crowd. I want you to make sure the rhythm section's on point," Even at that point when he was about to pass away, that's always been the biggest honor of my life. It always has.

Tony: Wasn't there supposed to be some sort of reunion tour with Flo and Eddie and, a lot of the older guys and yourself and things that never, came about?

Ike Willis: What happened was this. Right now I'm in Portland, Oregon, where I lived for 17 years. We moved up here after the last tour in '88. Frank went into remission. He called me around July of '93, and he'd been going through the prostate cancer thing, and suddenly he called me and said, hey, look, it seems like I'm in remission and I'm feeling better. I've got an idea of us doing the 25th anniversary of 200 Motels with Flo and Eddie, the London Philharmonic, and all sorts of folks, getting a few of the boys back together again and things like that. and on the following year, rehearsals were to begin then.

I was overjoyed. I was just thrilled. Then, of course, then in November of '93, he had a relapse, and then, the rest is history. He ended up passing away. Yes, that was going to be the big reunion tour, the big 200 Motels reunion tour and everything like that, and I was really looking forward to that because I'd never played with Flo and Eddie before and all that stuff. They were going to do the 88 tour. We actually rehearsed for like three days with Mark and Howard, and then that movie came out with Happy Together in it. Then they re-released Happy Together, and suddenly Flo and Eddie were big and famous again, and so they couldn't do the tour. Yes, I was looking. I had a chance at least to do three rehearsals with Mark and Howard, and, just amazing stuff, amazing stuff. Yes, in answer to the question, this was like something that we were both really looking forward to, and it just didn't end up happening.

Tony: Have you ever done anything with Dweezil and his band?

Ike Willis: No. I tried. Dweezil and I got together by phone because the second or third year of Zappa Plays Zappa, they got Ray White in the band, and Ray is like a part of the family. He's my son's godfather. We're like known as the Othello brothers, and Ray asked Dweezil and his manager if they, basically Ray wanted to do the Zappa Plays Zappa, but with the two of us. Dweezil and I discussed it, but it had to clear through Frank's, it had to clear through his mom, and that just didn't happen. That's, because Dweezil's my nephew. I love him to death. I've known him, when I joined the band, Dweezil was seven, Ahmet was five, Moon was nine, and Diva hadn't even been born yet. I would have loved playing with my nephew again. I really would have, that would have been great. It's fate, and it's just one of those things that didn't happen. We move on.

Tony: Maybe so. he's out there playing all the time. Maybe things will change at some point. That would be cool. I've gone and seen him a couple times. It's always a good show, and, of course, I've seen the other groups. I've seen Project Object a couple times. What other groups, do you get together with and play?

Ike Willis: Here's the thing. After Frank passed, a month later, I got started getting calls. I got a call from this band from Liverpool, The Muffin Men.

Tony: Right, of course.

Ike Willis: Which became my first Zappa tribute band.

Tony: I interviewed Reinhard Pruess. You know him, right?

Ike Willis: Reinhard Pruess, yes. He was our manager, and he owned Muffin Records. Basically, I joined The Muffin Men, went out on my first tour with them. Then toward the end of The Muffin Men tour, I recorded my first studio album with them. Then Reinhard asked me to see if I could get a hold of some of the veterans, like Arthur and the Fowler Brothers and Ed Mann and Tommy Mars, because there was a show in Stuttgart, the Stuttgart Jazz Open, and to see if I could convince the guys to do sort of like a reunion gig of the actual Zappa band. The main thing was, that's how we formed the band from Utopia.

Tony: I see.

Ike Willis: While I was still doing my first Muffin Men tour in 1994. We were basically, Artie, Tommy, Ed, Bruce Fowler, and myself, we formed the band from Utopia. We came back and did the Stuttgart Jazz Open, which is actually still making the rounds on the Internet and YouTube and things like that. Then we toured with Reinhard Pruess as our manager for Muffin Records. That's how Band from Utopia was formed. Band from Utopia became my second Zappa Tribute band. Then after Band From Utopia,. Then came Project Object. Then I had an Italian Zappa Tribute band called O.C. Dory based in Turin. Then there's another one based in Brazil and in Sao Paulo called the Central Scrutinizer Band, which I'm going to be playing with in October, along with Bobby and Ray. Then Bogus Pump in Florida. There's so many! Let's see. Bogus Pump in Florida. Then there's Ugly Radio Rebellion, the Ed Palermo Big Band. Basically, I lose track. I lose count.

Fast forward, my 11th band, actually I've got some guys in New Jersey, some kids, some conservatory kids that are based in New Jersey and Philadelphia over the last year who became my 11th Zappa Tribute band. They're called We Used To Cut The Grass, who are also going to be the Ike Willis Project on the East Coast. Then the 12th band is… I forgot already. It'll come back to me. I've been pretty – they keep me pretty busy. Over the years, I managed to accumulate now up to 12 Zappa Tribute bands, Project Object being, my number one Zappa Tribute band because I basically was with them the longest, even though the Muffin Man, actually we just hit our almost, 20 years, just about 20 years with the Muffins. Oh yea… my 12th Zappa Tribute band is called Zapatica. They're based in Leiden, Holland. I just got back from touring with those guys last month.

Tony: It keeps you busy. you don't want to sit at home and do nothing. With all these groups playing all the time, I guess there's no shortage of gigs for you.

Ike Willis: That's the thing. It's all a matter of scheduling. All of these different bands are totally independent bands run by their own band leaders. They're in different countries and different states and different cities all over the world. It depends on what my schedule is, what their schedule is, and what their individual, day jobs are. you get the idea. Everybody, because they've got wives and kids and lives! My Italian kids, Ossi Duria, when I joined the band, the youngest member of the band was 11 years old. He's like a miniature Vinnie Colaiuta. They know everything. These kids are so damn incredibly proficient musicians that, my main guys, I've been with these guys for over 15 years, That's the thing. these kids are, well, I used to be the younger guy in the band when I joined Zappa. Now I'm the old coot, I'm the old man.

Tony: Right.

Ike Willis: In fact, I just became a grandfather last Saturday. My youngest, Leah, she and her hubby just had our first grandchild. I'm still wrapping my head around being the old guy,

Tony: I've seen the grandmothers a couple of times. Any dealings with any of those guys? They're doing different era stuff.

Ike Willis: Actually, I'm a founding member of the grandmothers as well.

Tony: Wow!

Ike Willis: Because I used to play with the Fowler brothers. I joined Frank in 78, and in 79, I met Tom Fowler. The rest of the Fowler brothers, they had a band called Air Pocket. They used to tour up and down the West Coast. Chester Thompson, who also was Frank Zappa's drummer, his wife, Roz, were in Air Pocket. Then when Roz got pregnant, Tom Fowler asked me to replace Roz on lead vocals. This was in 79. I had been playing with Air

Pocket for years and years and years. Then in 81, we formed the grandmothers with Jimmy Carl Black, Buzz Gardner, Tony Duran, Motorhead Sherwood. It was like Air Pocket and the old mothers and the Frank Zappa band, This was like a combination of three eras of Zappa. Which was really great.

Tony: Let's talk about your solo albums. You've got a couple of albums out, which I know people can get on Amazon.com. I looked it up. Just type in your name on CD Baby.

Ike Willis: Also on my website, ikewillis.com as well.

Tony: Are you putting like tour dates or things where you're going to be up there so people can maybe go out to see you?

Ike Willis: I do! I have put together my new band, the Ike Willis Project. It's no longer the Ike Willis Band. I've already begun work on my third solo album, finally. I know that people have been asking me for years. My manager, Hank Woods, and I are starting to plan to do some West and East Coast tour dates. Actually, we're in the process of doing that now, so keep your fingers crossed.

Tony: Yes. It sounds like things are happening. That's great. You're doing the solo project stuff yourself. That's great, too. A lot of people are just doing the Zappa stuff, and that's it. That's cool, a nice combination of both.

Ike Willis: I've been doing it for so long. Basically, I started doing this in '94. Okay? I essentially started doing this myself in '94 because Frank asked me to help keep his music alive. He said, whatever way that I could possibly do that to make that happen, then do it. I had his permission, which is what I've been doing.

Essentially, once I got that first phone call from the Muffins in '94, I've been luckier than most. I've been very lucky and very blessed at the fact that Frank's fans are intensely loyal. Okay, let me start there. They're intensely loyal. I know fans of his that I met when I was 20 years old, now they have great grandchildren. Okay? Let me put it that way. They are loyal. They come to the shows. They support everything that we do. I also get to fulfill Frank's request to me. that's the main thing. He asked me to do this, and I'm doing it.

ED MANN

Ed Mann is a musician primarily known for his work as a percussionist and marimba player. He is perhaps best recognized for his extensive collaboration with the American composer and musician Frank Zappa. Mann's association with Zappa began in the late 1970s and continued through the 1980s. He performed on numerous Zappa albums and toured with Zappa's band.

Mann's contribution to Zappa's music was significant, particularly in live performances where his percussion skills added depth and complexity to Zappa's intricate compositions. After Zappa's passing in 1993, Mann continued to be involved in various musical projects and collaborations.

In addition to his work with Zappa, Mann has also participated in other musical endeavors, including recording and performing with his own groups and other artists. His versatile skills as a percussionist have earned him respect within the music industry.

Tony. How are you? Where are you at now? What part of the country are you in?

Ed Mann: I'm in Massachusetts right now.

Tony: Massachusetts. Where do you live?

Ed Mann: I've been in Northern California the last couple of years.

Tony: I think that I read, Santa Rosa?

Ed Mann: Around Santa Rosa, yes.

Tony: Massachusetts? Are you playing over there? What are you doing?

Ed Mann: Actually, I did just play a bunch of gigs with this band, Z3. Great band.

Tony: Z3, it sounds like...

Ed Mann: It's an organ trio, and they play all Zappa. They're really exceptional musicians, these guys, and great improvisers.

Tony: I think I've seen a video on them. The guy plays a B3, along with a guitar player and drummer.

Ed Mann: We did four shows. It was great, adding the mallets and percussion to that. Taking a lot of freedom with the tunes, a ton of freedom, and reinventing them.

Tony: As I saw on your Facebook page, you're into the Mallet Cat, which I love that thing. I saw you've got a Launch Pad and a Chaos Pad. It looks great!

Ed Mann: Yes, it's fun.

Tony: What's your opinion on... I've been a percussionist since junior high, and I just couldn't find a lot of work for it.

Ed Mann: Nothing's changed.

Tony: Yes, right.

Ed Mann: Except, no, that's not true, because of drumline and field stuff. That didn't exist 40 years ago.

Tony: Yes, I remember being on the drumline in high school and dragging the marimba across the field. What a nightmare that was.

Ed Mann: Yes. Probably... With the choices and instruments, just having to schlep is a major thing to think about as you plan your activities and your career. You don't want to be schlepping that much.

Tony: Throw that Mallet Cat right in the suitcase, and away you go.

Ed Mann: That's right. It's fantastic, especially in LA.

Tony: How do you feel about that though... it's all electronic. I think there's something nice about hitting a real piece of wood. The benefits, I can see, outweigh dragging all that stuff around. Do you miss the old days with tons of stuff around you?

Ed Mann: Yes and no. it was a unique and rare situation to be able to have that opportunity,

Tony: With Frank.

Ed Mann: Yes. Having enough people to move stuff like that on a daily basis and not having to be responsible for setting up, which means now I can play well. If I had to be the one setting it all up, I wouldn't play well after that.

Tony: Yes, right.

Ed Mann: I don't miss it because that was then and this is now. I've been playing on a real vibraphone up until a couple years ago, and that's great. Then there's limitations in terms of sound and the range of the actual instrument, which I love being able to access from the Mallet Cat. Ultimately, you just go for the music. If you're able to get the music out there, then that, for me, seems to override any particular thing about, I wish it was real metal or real wood, versus just having triggers. And plus now I can do pitch bends and I can do ring modulation and do all this crazy stuff with the sound, which is, for a percussionist's way of thinking, fantastic. That's what you want. You want to be able to explore as many permutations of the sound as possible.

Tony: Right.

Ed Mann: It's just different, I would say. I'm thankful for it because if it wasn't for that, I wouldn't be playing very much right now, not live.

Tony: I like how the Mallet Cat offers the pieces that go in between the notes, so when you miss and you whack the case! I see you're not using those. I wouldn't assume you'd miss too many times, but I know I would. If I'm going to buy one of those things, I'm having all the protection I want because, it looks pretty bad if you're hitting the case.

Ed Mann: It's a nice thing because it's super loud if it hits the case. It's so loud. It's just deafening.

Tony: I've been threatening to buy one for years, and now I think I've just GOT to go out and get one.

Ed Mann: I would highly recommend it. The other reason for that is, for me at least, it really helps in developing creativity. Writing, composing. Because it's the tool that goes right in between your imagination and documenting the event, Recording it in MIDI or in audio. Having that, like having it hooked up to a laptop and always recording everything you do is really helps a lot in terms of staying, dynamic and vibrant as a composer, as a creative thinker.

Tony: I know that you first appeared on Live in New York. I think you did some overdubs because Ruth Underwood was in the band then. I guess that led to you being in the band later. How did that happen?

Ed Mann: I met Ruth and I stayed in touch with her. Then Frank called Ruth one night because he couldn't find a second keyboard player. Ruth called me because she knew that I knew some interesting people. I knew Tommy Mars. I thought, yes, I have just the guy, Then that led to joining the band.

Tony: I know that Ruth was with him for, years and years. Then what, she just got tired of being on the road?

Ed Mann: Yes, I heard something like that.

Tony: It's great for you!

Ed Mann: I know, it's ridiculous. I wasn't really a mallet player when I got the job. I messed around on mallets. It was not a hobby, but I was supporting myself as a drummer and as a percussionist. It was just unlikely. I don't know, still don't know really why I got the gig.

Tony: You got real good. real fast then, if that's the case, because...

Ed Mann: Yes, there's nothing like fear to motivate you, I was thinking "This is unbelievable, this is ridiculous." I had Ruth Underwood's job. It was like a bizarre dream, just so unlikely.

Tony: You don't still have those Syndrums around, do you? Because if you do, I want to buy them!

Ed Mann: I just sold the last ones.

Tony: I like that crazy disco-y sound... I look on eBay all the time, I'm trying to find some. Either they're so broken up that you don't want them or whatever. It's the classic Sheik Yerbouti sound that's everywhere on that album... and I just can't get enough of it.

Ed Mann: That's great because when we were doing that, I was saying to myself, I can't believe he's decided to put this much Syndrums everywhere. We did it on one tune and Frank said, "Okay, now, next tune." It was just like, okay, another tune, another tune. Just fill it up with Syndrums because it was unique and he was having fun with it. Even me at that time, I thought "this is way too much." I haven't really listened to the release that carefully enough to hear them all over the place, so I assume most of it is there. Yes, it's just like a signature for that record, I guess.

Tony: Only that album though, It never showed up much on any other album that I've ever heard. Not like that, maybe occasionally...

Ed Mann: That's just a great example of Frank. If he loves something, he'll go completely overboard with it. That just happened to be the moment. The thing that made the Syndrums great and unique was the fact that you had eight sliders per drum. You could change the sweep, you could hit the tone and have it sustaining and then change the LFO and then speed up the LFO and do all kinds of stuff in real time in order to tailor the sound event. You can recreate that right now with any laptop program and then a dedicated controller that gave you eight faders, like the Akai thing.

Tony: Right. Yes, I got it.

Ed Mann: Just assign them to those same parameters and you could have then effectively the same thing.

Tony: When you start getting Zappa charts, like the Black Page and whatever. How do you handle that stuff? Was that like, yes, I can read that no problem or was that just hours and hours of practice?

Ed Mann: Most of the stuff doesn't require hours and hours of practice. Most of the stuff just requires playing it a few times to see what it is and then getting it in your ear. Then in every chart there's always a couple bars that will take days of practice. Going back to it, because you're having to retrain your hands and arms to move in ways that are not natural and to execute these events. It's like quantum mallet. It's where your mallet is literally in two places at the same time to execute some of these things.

Tony: You were jumping back and forth between instruments like crazy.

Ed Mann: That's the thing. That jumping around from instrument to instrument, those aren't Frank's ideas. Those are my ideas. He just told me to put stuff where I thought it worked best and that I could have freedom and liberty with it if I wanted to harmonize something, If I wanted to edit a part and only play sections of it or just put the last two notes of a passage over on one instrument. Whatever I wanted to do, just do it. The only way to do that is to have it in memory. Now you can have fun with it.

Tony: That's great to know because that adds a lot to the way you would play it as compared to somebody else who would play it completely different.

Ed Mann: What he would come in with was just simple charts. If it was a melody, a single line melody, everybody got the same melody and then you start to work with it and, work with the raw material.

Tony: On the Baby Snakes film, you have a ton of stuff. Was that yours? Was that Frank's? Who owned all that stuff?

Ed Mann: That was mostly mine. The chimes were Frank's and the big bass drum was Frank's. The vibes at that time were

Frank's. Everything else was mine. Gradually then, by the end, by '88, it was all mine. By '82, actually, it was all mine. Yes, '81. I replaced his vibe with my vibe. I just bought a lot of stuff. By '82, we had turned, by the end of '79 or '78, we had turned everything electric. The gongs, the gong pickups happened in '81, but everything except the gongs. The xylophone had pickups on it. The temple bell, temple block had pickups. The cowbell had pickups. Everything had pickups. piezos, piezo elements.

Tony: I saw a thing online with Ruth where Frank actually said, I'm going to drill into the marimba here and we're going to add little pickups. She was like, "Really? You're going to drill into these?"

Ed Mann: Yes, that's how it's done.

Tony: Yes, that's a big jump.

Ed Mann: It doesn't really affect the sound there, though.

Tony: I see.

Ed Mann: It's right where the rope passes through. Otherwise, it would totally affect the sound.

Tony: I got halfway decent playing with two mallets, but all the real players in the world, use four..

Ed Mann: I don't know, man. Listen to Bobby Hutcherson. That's about as real as you get.

Tony: He's a two-mallet player.

Ed Mann: You can do certain things with two mallets that you cannot do with four. That has to do with real fast ornamentation and extended glissandos, controlled glissandos. I call it a glissando, but it's actually more like arpeggios played like they're an ornament. it's an afterthought or leading into a main event. That density, at least for me, I can do that a lot easier with two mallets than four mallets. I play mostly two mallets. I'll grab four mallets if I need it. But if I don't need it, I'll stay on two because it's more like drumming.

Tony: Are you seeing a lot of really hot, new, younger people coming up playing mallet percussions?

Ed Mann: Yes. it's like anything else where there's young players now that just wouldn't have existed when I was young because the bar hadn't been set that high. Yes. it's like...

Tony: It was set that high by you. Sorry.

Ed Mann: I'm one in the string!

Tony: Right, of course.

Ed Mann: When Terry Bozio played the Black Page on the drums, people thought that it was impossible. But Terry figured it out. It took him half a year, but he figured it out. Then another guy did, and now it's standard. Now everywhere you go, you hear people playing the Black Page. No problem. Because there's something about seeing somebody else do it helps you get what it's all about. This is how I would approach it, this is how I would play it. Anyway, I hear players now that are just amazing.

Tony: Who's the guy with Dweezil?

Ed Mann: The first guy with Dweezil was Billy Holton. I heard him when he was younger, I realized, wow, that's way ahead of where we were in 1974.

Tony: Wow...

Ed Mann: It's like the generations keep getting better and better and better.

Tony: Right. Of course. I mean, look at young Eddy Van Halen He was amazing, and he invented a bunch of stuff, and nobody else could do that. Now years later, every 14-year-old with a guitar can play like that. Only ONE person invented that style of playing. It's like learning The Black Page first.

Ed Mann: Bozio was a first in that way.

Tony: You were in a band with Tommy Mars way back in the early '70s, right?

Ed Mann: Yea, It was covers. A lot of Chick Corea at the time, especially the first Return to Forever was a huge influence on it. We had some originals, but we were mostly focused on reinventing this other material that we liked.

Tony: You've actually gone out and played a little bit with Project Object and Band From Utopia and all those guys?

Ed Mann: Yes, I did. We just got done with the Band From Utopia thing that was real successful. It was in Europe, of course, and that was in November, and it just came off better than we ever could have anticipated. That seems to have some energy around it. We're going to do more in April and hope to do the United States someday. Then there's a local band here in New England, Z3.

Tony: Z3, yes.

Ed Mann: I do my own things here and there. I'm getting ready to start doing my own thing, which is completely different than any of that stuff. Again, like jazz, like tribal jazz.

Tony: Tribal jazz. Cool.

Ed Mann: Groove, ambient, dub jazz thing.

Tony: I don't know what Frank actually considered himself, a rock guy, a composer, a jazz guy. What do you think?

Ed Mann: He knew that he was a music guy. Right. I don't think he ever had any internal dialogue about that. Just anything. He was authentic in any genre that he approached. You can hear it in the music. He's absolutely an authentic rock guy. An authentic jazz guy. You listen to the recordings of what he was doing with The Grand Wazoo.

Tony: Right.

Ed Mann: That is amazing. it's so jazz. Yes, of course. it really is, and stands up to any of the stuff. For me, it stands up to any of the Thelonious Monk live recordings or any of those great eclectic composers. The orchestral stuff is absolutely authentic 20th century contemporary orchestral writing, without a doubt.

Tony: Yes, I don't know of too many other people that could pull off writing so many different styles.

Ed Mann: There's nobody. Zap is an original. He's like, he is to composition what Hendrix is to the electric guitar. There was no one before him like that. There's been no one since. Unlikely that there will be. Not in Frank's case. Not that's that prolific. He was so well versed in so many styles and can connect the humanity of it all to the musical prowess.

Tony: AND to make it funny at the same time! To have a sense of humor when you're trying to do all that really complex stuff. That's just amazing. Yea, no one will ever pull that off.

Ed Mann: Then to be also such an interesting electric guitarist, unique. Great guitarist.

Tony: Yes.

Ed Mann: In his own category in that way, too. There's no one that plays like him and developed that style.

Tony: All the guitar players like the high little notes and he liked the low ones. Those solos using lower notes than you never hear a guitar player play. There's a style all its own. I know I've heard Steve Vai do things that were fantastic and sound very close to that. You can tell it's not the same person. Dweezil too. It's like pretty close, but that's a hard one to imitate.

Ed Mann: Only Frank thought that way.

MIKE KENEALLY

Mike Keneally is a highly versatile and accomplished musician, known for his proficiency as a guitarist, keyboardist, vocalist, and composer. He gained prominence for his work as a member of Frank Zappa's band in the late 1980s and early 1990s. Keneally's tenure with Zappa allowed him to showcase his exceptional musical abilities and contributed to his recognition as a standout talent in the world of progressive and experimental rock.

Following his time with Zappa, Keneally pursued a diverse solo career, releasing numerous albums that span a wide range of musical styles, including rock, jazz, fusion, and avant-garde. His solo work often showcases his virtuosic guitar playing, intricate compositions, and eclectic influences.

In addition to his solo career, Keneally has collaborated with a variety of artists and bands, both as a performer and a producer. He has worked with musicians such as Steve Vai, Joe Satriani, Devin Townsend, and Dweezil Zappa, among others. Keneally's contributions to the music world extend beyond his own recordings.

Tony: You were with Frank from '88 through about '06 or…?

Mike Keneally: Only the front part of that was with Frank because he stopped playing in '88, and then I went on to play with Dweezil for about six years.

Tony: How did you get into Frank's band to begin with?

Mike Keneally: I called him up and asked for a job!

Tony: Yes. He said "Come in and audition."

Mike Keneally: Yes, well, it stemmed from hearing the announcement that he was back in rehearsal with a band in late '87. That was big news. That was surprising information because he had said after the '84 tour that he wasn't going to tour anymore. When I heard that announcement, I thought, well, that's amazing. As a fan, I was just excited to hear that he was going to play again, but then I thought that it might serve me well to be a little more ambitious and see about getting in the band because he was absolutely it for me when I was developing musically. I probably logged more hours listening to his music than anyone else's music as I was sort of becoming who I was. He had a huge impact on me and it was always a dream to work with him.

Tony: That's fantastic.

Mike Keneally: I just went for it.

Tony: Did he make you transcribe things as an audition piece?

Mike Keneally: No, he learned early on that transcription was not a strong suit for me. It wasn't because I had no formal musical training to speak of. I did have a few years of organ lessons, so that was a very specific genre and a very specific direction. Anything beyond that I learned about modern music or composition or transcription or any of that, it was just basically self-taught trial and error.

I definitely did not have conservatory-trained Steve Vai-like transcription skills at that point in my life. What was more useful to Frank was just the fact that I knew the catalog so well and that I had a lot of the songs tucked away in my memory banks so that if he decided he wanted to try something, there was a better than average chance that I would know the structure and be able to help piece the arrangement together. He discovered at that first audition when he put the chord chart for *Yo Cats* in front of me..

Tony: You guys practiced for like eight hours a day for a couple of months or something, didn't you?

Mike Keneally: Four months, five days a week, eight hours a day.

Tony: Now, did you work with Arthur Barrow?

Mike Keneally: No, he wasn't there while we were there.

Tony: I see.

Mike Keneally: I'm trying to recall if I ever even met Arthur. If so, it was definitely fleeting. Right. I think he's a great guy, but I don't think we've hung much.

Tony: Now, you just did a gig with another guy I talked to, Ed Palermo. What did you do there?

Mike Keneally: I really get a kick out of Ed's arrangements. I think he does a nice job with the music. Every few years, he'll just get in touch out of the blue and say, "You want to come and be a special guest for a few shows?" It's really exhilarating to be on stage while those arrangements are happening. I do get a huge kick out of performing with Ed. It's a really good time.

Tony: You can just tell that he is an arranger. That's what he calls himself in life, I think. I'm sure he gets a big kick out of doing those arrangements, throwing other songs in there. He was telling me about some of the things that he does. It sounds great. I actually have to go to New York and see him play.

Mike Keneally: Yes, he'll just do these sort of fascinating – he'll make these connections in his mind and see how this ELP song might connect with this Wayne Shorter theme, which might connect with this Zappa thing. It's all incredibly top-notch music. The way he handles it is really creative and really respectful and really skilled. His chops as an arranger are pretty out of this world. I just have a lot of respect for what he does.

Tony: I tried to look up the albums that you've put out. I got tired of writing them all down!. You have so many.

Mike Keneally: So far... I haven't been stopped! No one's put a stop to it, so I just keep going.

Tony: Now what's the Sluggo project? Is that their latest one?

Mike Keneally: That's the latest release, although it's based on an album that was originally released in '97. That was when Sluggo first came out. It's an original mix. Then I switched record labels. The original Sluggo, went out of print in the early part of the 2000s. It hasn't been available on CD for a real long time. It was an album that fans were really taken with. There are a lot of songs from that album that became core pieces of the live repertoire that I still play. There's a lot of good feelings for that record. It hasn't been available on physical media for a super long time. We started talking about reissuing it. I realized that I always had my personal problems with the original mix, the way that it went down, because we did that album during breaks.\

I was in Steve Vai's band at the time. We were working on Sluggo in breaks in the schedule of Steve's touring schedule. These days I'm used to making albums in sort of piecemeal fashion over a long period of time. Back then it was really disconcerting. We also had a deadline that we were adhering to. We had one mix that didn't work out. We just had a few days to do a second mix and master. That's the one that went out. I've always been really happy with the songs on the album, but not that happy with the way it sounds.

We went back and did a new stereo mix, including a new surround mix. It sounds miles better than it ever sounded before. We also have about three hours of video in the package. It's a three-disc package that's just like Sluggo overload. It's really nice. There's also a super deluxe version that has an additional live CD of us in '98 at a place in Boston called *Mama Kim* that turned out to be a really great gig. It's a very elaborate package with a lot of material in there.

Tony: People can just go on Amazon and all the stuff is there. Are you doing hard copies or is it just all downloads anymore?

Mike Keneally: We have a real fondness for physical media still. We try to do nice things with packaging and to make it worthwhile to have this thing in your house.

Tony: That's fantastic, the way it should be, the way it always was until just recently. Do you record everything at the house like, most people do nowadays? Do you go out to other studios?

Mike Keneally: Various albums get recorded in various locations. The stuff that I'm working on these days for the most part is up in the northern part of San Diego, about a half hour north of where I live.

Tony: Yes, I think that's where I saw you on the video. Now you've got an album out with Steve Vai... Piano Reductions. What's that one?

Mike Keneally: That was after I had been in his band for a couple of years. He had this idea that he wanted to put out a solo piano album of various of his own compositions that he thought would be well suited to a solo piano format. He gave me a list of

11 tracks that he wanted me to arrange and perform on piano. Steve gave me this list of songs, and it took me a long time to do the arrangements, and then I gave him multiple takes of each song. Then he spent several years editing together his favorite sections of the performances and then finally, about five years after it was recorded, it came out in 2004 as Vai Piano Reductions, Volume 1. Although I don't know if I will ever be able to find time to do a Volume 2, because it really was one of the most incredibly difficult and complex and soul-challenging projects I've ever been a part of, but I was really happy to have done it.

I like the idea of taking Steve's melodies, which are frequently beautiful melodies, and highlighting them in a different format. Because everyone is so focused on Steve as both a guitar player and, in some cases, people prejudge him on that basis. For some reason, guitarists have, a lot of people have negative feelings about guitar players. That's too bad. To take just the basic material that he wrote and put that in a piano situation is what I think was interesting for a lot of people. Steve was very happy with the way it turned out, and I was happy with the way it turned out.

Tony: It's great. I've been playing the drums for a lot of years, but I think I've made more money as a keyboard player just because maybe it's easier to replace the drummer than it is to replace the keyboard player! I always thought that was funny, somebody making their living, say, as a guitar player, but then, being a keyboard player just because you almost have to nowadays. I don't know. I like both instruments.

Mike Keneally: I started on keyboard when I was seven and then moved to guitar when I was 11. Frank hired me as a keyboardist as well as a guitar player, so they've always both been a part of my thing. It's just that I, at some point, became more well-known as a guitar player. Then Joe Satriani hired me for his band. He initially hired me just as a keyboard player. For the first three years that I was in Satriani's band, a lot of his audience who had never seen me before just thought of me as a keyboardist. During this last year, when I started playing guitar as well with Satriani, that suddenly, it was like people were surprised. They're like, look, the keyboard player is playing guitar. It's funny. My career has gone through different stages that way.

Tony: Now, you guys are doing the G4 experience in August, right? That's coming up soon.

Mike Keneally: It's actually a music camp. It's going to be four days of some pretty serious musical thinking and musical playing. We're going to have seminars during the day and classes, and then there'll be jams at night. It'll just be a very concentrated musical environment for a few days. It's focused on the guitar, so it's going to be, I'm sure, a pretty deep experience.

Tony: Is that open still for people to get in, or has that been closed up for a while?

Mike Keneally: Yes. as far as I know, tickets are definitely still available.

Tony: Okay.

Mike Keneally: I think there are different tiers of, you can get housing on site and stuff like that. People should check out the G4 Experience website if they're interested in that.

Tony: Any good Frank Zappa stories that you've got that I might not know about or something that happened in the band?

Mike Keneally: I swear to you, and I apologize in advance, I'm the worst for just, dragging up anecdotes. For whatever reason, I need some prompting. It's like nothing comes to mind. It's awful. Part of the problem is just the way my brain works. I'm definitely in the moment. Then, when I move on to the next thing, I've sort of let go of the last thing.

Tony: With Frank, were you on any studio recordings, or was it all the live stuff?

Mike Keneally: All live stuff. He did manage to get a lot of releases out of the live recordings, because it was five discs worth of live material, plus scattered things on Y*ou can't do it on stage anymore*, and some tracks on *Transfusion*. Considering we never went in the studio, he did manage to find a lot of releasable stuff from that tour, which was cool.

Tony: A lot of the guys that I talked to only did studio work, they didn't go out and play much at all.

Mike Keneally: Yes, I would have loved to have worked more with Frank in the studio. I guess the only thing I did which I guess could qualify as a studio recording was for his birthday one year, I went to his place, and I played the acoustic guitar piece *Sleep Dirt.*

Tony: Right.

Mike Keneally: Yes, I played that on his Synclavier, so that he could record it and orchestrate it. Then a few months later, I went to the house, and he said, do you remember when you played *Sleep Dirt* on the keyboard? Then he played me the orchestration that he had done of that performance, and it was super cool. That's still in the vault somewhere.

Tony: I hear there's a lot of things in that vault that I guess they're working on little by little to get out, but I...

Mike Keneally: It's insane the amount of stuff they have over there. I've been delighted by the stuff that's been coming out. it's been a pretty hectic release schedule that they've been adhering to, and I think that Joe Travers is doing an amazing job with finding things to release. I'm very happy with the schedule of recordings. I thought *Joe's Camouflage* was really cool. I think the *Road Tapes* releases were extraordinarily cool. They just keep pumping out the stuff. I think it's great.

Tony: They release all that bootleg stuff. I thought that was a great idea. You get bootleg stuff, you just round it up and package it yourself and sell it.

Mike Keneally: I think that was sort of trailblazing. I think there have probably been similar releases, but never presented in such a clear fashion. It's like, okay, here's the bootlegs, and I'm going to just repackage them and make them more easily available. Since then, a lot of bands have done similar things. I do think Frank plays the trail there.

Tony: You went and played with Dweezil in the band. I had no idea.

Mike Keneally: Yes. Originally, it was just called the Dweezil Zappa Band. Then around '93, I think, the name of the band changed to Z. That was a full-time gig for a number of years.

Tony: The son plays the dad's music. I think it's fantastic!

Mike Keneally: The only thing that I think is a little sad is that Dweezil's own music gets short shrift as a result. A lot of people maybe are not as aware of some of the stuff that Dweezil was doing in the early '90s, which was the shows, especially the live shows of the Dweezil's Zappa Band and then Z, were some of the most interesting and challenging performances I've ever been a part of. The level of musicianship was insanely high. The shows were just, intense and exhilarating. Unfortunately, it went to a certain point and stopped. I also think it was difficult for us to capture the intensity of the live band on the studio albums.

Man, some of those early Dweezil and Z gigs were just really intense and satisfying shows. People would just be really blown away. I wish more people knew about that. Ahmet was the front man of that band. He was somebody that I think was a trailblazer in a way. He had a live persona on stage that I saw come out more in other performers years later. The first time I saw Jack Black, I thought. man, he's doing Ahmet. It just so happened that Ahmet had a performance style that, again, was almost like a parody of show business. At the same time that it was really, intelligently done and expertly done. He also went from zero to 60 as a vocalist.

Dweezil just said "Okay, you're going to be my lead singer." He had to work out what that meant. What was being asked of him vocally was really challenging. He would just go out there and kill it. Yes, it was a cool band. Scott Thunes was in that band. Then Josh Freeze was the original drummer. Josh went on to play with a million people. He plays a lot with Nine Inch Nails and just like studio drummer par excellence. Josh and Scott left. Joe Travers came in the band. Her ended up being in my band after the Dweezil band stopped. I've had a long-time association with Joe Travers ever since then. That was, like the flash point for a lot of stuff.

Tony: You have Keneally.com. That's great.

Mike Keneally: We've had the website for 20 years now.

Tony: Lucky to get it!

Mike Keneally: You've got to be in under the wire early on! I didn't even know what the internet or website was! Yes, 20 years now we've had that website going.

LISA POPEIL

Lisa Popeil is a renowned vocal coach, singer, and expert in vocal technique. She is the creator of the Voiceworks® method, which integrates vocal science with practical techniques to help singers improve their vocal abilities. Popeil has been involved in the music industry for decades, working with a wide range of artists, from beginners to professionals, to help them develop and maintain healthy, strong, and versatile voices.

In addition to her work as a vocal coach, Popeil is also an accomplished singer and performer. She has appeared on numerous recordings, commercials, and television shows, showcasing her own vocal talents. As an educator, Popeil has conducted workshops, seminars, and masterclasses worldwide, sharing her knowledge and expertise in vocal technique with aspiring singers and voice teachers.

Popeil's contributions to the field of vocal instruction have been widely recognized, and she is considered a leading authority on vocal health, technique, and performance.

Tony: Hey, Lisa, are you there?

Lisa Popeil: I'm here, Tony.

Tony: Thanks for being on the show here with me. Now, I'm in Nashville, Tennessee. Where are you? Are you still in Los Angeles?

Lisa Popeil: I am. I'm in Los Angeles, and I'd like to tell you how it's 85 today, but it isn't. It's actually our typical winter weather here, which is in the 60s. It's been strangely warm and as enjoyable as it's been, it has seemed a bit apocalyptic as we're hearing what's going on in the rest of the country.

Tony: I can't ignore this, though, that you are a – you're a Popeil, of the famous Popeil people! You're one degree away of separation from the pocket fisherman!

Lisa Popeil: One degree! My dad, who passed away in '84, was the creator of the pocket fisherman, and the Vegematic. He had over 200 patents by the time of his death. He had a factory. He was a manufacturer. He started it in the '40s. It's such an interesting story of starting with little and ending up with being an icon of American marketing. It's his son, Ron, who's my half-brother, who really took it and actually came out with new, improved versions of the pocket fisherman and Vegematic. Ron is still pushing and clicking and creating. He's been working on his most recent project now for six, seven, eight years now. He's like me. We love to work and solve problems.

Tony: Every time... back a few years ago... you'd turn on the TV and there he was. Does he do the TV gig anymore or is it different?

Lisa Popeil: It's different now because he sold his company a few years ago. That company may still be running some of the old infomercials. Ron is not active now in doing infomercials or being on QVC. You never know. I can see him doing it again. I really can. With new product, I could see him saying "I'm just going to do it myself." I could see him doing it again.

Tony: He also made an item that I had… the *Mr. Microphone*. Hold on. Let me say the line. "Hey, baby. We'll be back to pick you up later!" It actually transmitted to the FM signal of your car radio. What a great idea!

Lisa Popeil: What about the smokeless ashtray? The egg scrambler. You didn't have to crack an egg and be grossed out. Mix it yourself. The thing I thought was so funny was the egg scrambler was on the packaging. It was called cordless electric. Yes, right. It's a fancy way to say batteries.

Tony: Batteries. Yes, sure.

Lisa Popeil: That makes me laugh.

Tony: That's marketing. See, you could say this is a battery operated and batteries are not included. Sorry, it's cordless electric.

Lisa Popeil: Yes, it sounds like you're getting so much more.

Tony: On to a little bit more about you. I tried to keep up and read a little bit about what you've done. In '84 you did your self-titled album. Is that available? Can I buy that somewhere? How would someone go about getting something like that?

Lisa Popeil: I have a few left. My collector's items, I destroyed so many of them. They're quite horrible, but I love the cover. I think the cover, which I actually have more to do with, I think looks great. I do have a few. If anyone wants to contact me through my website, I'm happy to talk to them after I try to talk them out of getting it!

If I were to be an artist now, I'd have a much clearer idea on how to do it and how to be good. I was just starting out. I'd worked with Frank in '81 and performed with him in December of '81. Then '83, started to work on an album with a friend of mine, a producer who was an avaunt-gard jazz producer. I wasn't really ready to do an album, but my mother was so excited by the performance she saw me do with Frank that she said, That's it. It's your time. I wasn't quite ready. I didn't have a real clear sense of direction. The album is a mishmash of too many styles. It was a huge learning experience for me.

I learned everything about making an album, marketing, at least as the '80s. It was a huge experience. I made a music video. It led to a small record deal. That was in '84. It was the beginning of a period of learning about how the business works. It all started with just being at the right place at the right time.

I didn't know much about Frank Zappa's music. I went to Cal Arts. I got my master's degree in voice. There were a number of guys I went to school with who worked for Frank, whether it was transcriptions or drum tech, guitar tech. My drummer boyfriend at the time was a Zappa fan, and he had heard about the auditions coming up for the '81 tour. I was happy to go and help him set up his drums and give him some moral support. I had no other expectations than that. It was a really bizarre and memorable experience for me because I remember being overweight and wearing these ugly red shorts and this little white top with little hearts on it.

When we went to the studio, I just watched one talented person come in after another and get thrown out mercilessly. I thought, wow, this is low. I'm not used to that. There was some music sitting around and I would just glance at it. If I have a gift, it's sight singing and sight reading keyboards. That's just my talent. My talent is not memorizing music because I can just read. I've been playing piano since I was four and my memory's never been that great anyway. I was getting ready to leave and Tommy Mars said "Can you read that?" I said "Yes, I can." You can read that. He said "You should audition for Frank." I said "I don't know"... So I did, and I sat down for my audition at the keyboard at the nine foot grand with the extension, which was very impressive.

Frank kept testing me. He was an amazing tester. He knew exactly what aspects of musical skill to test. He'd bring out this piece of music. He'd say "Now play that. Now sing this. Now put this together." I had a few little tricks up my sleeve to sound like I could improvise more than I really could. It sounded like I really knew what I was doing. I was there for probably at the keyboard for 45 minutes. I turned around and I saw an increasingly large group of people standing behind me with their mouths hanging open.

I was 25, just gotten out of college and didn't have any plans. They were just staring at me like, what is she doing here? Because I could just do these things. Then I stood up and sang some things. Frank said "Well, come back on Monday. It's like four days. Here's a stack of music. Learn it. Come back on Monday." I just practiced as much as I could and memorized as much as I could from scratch. Really, I had not heard this music before. I came back on Monday and did my best. I was not in the band for a trial period. Then it got much harder. Much harder.

Tony: I'll bet!

Lisa Popeil: My goal with him was always to make him laugh because I knew how to make him laugh. I knew how to do weird things with my voice that would just tickle him. If he could fall off his stool at rehearsals, then I know that I had done something good with my life. I was only in the band for three weeks of intense work, hardly sleeping and practicing a lot!. Every moment I was awake, my hands were swollen. Only time in my life that my hands have swelled from sitting at the keyboard practicing. I did perform with him and it was a real highlight of my life. It felt like that's where I should be. It felt completely natural to get on stage and feel like the audience was a huge hand that was just reaching out to me. It was magical for me. I'm so thankful that I have that opportunity to perform and do my thing for thousands of people. I still have people contact me all the time and still enjoy the recordings that were made from that live performance.

Tony: Now you didn't do any more. You just didn't want to go on the road?

Lisa Popeil: No, he replaced me! He really needed someone on the tour that was experienced. This was the beginning of synth keyboards. I was a piano player. To learn four hours of music, to be able to play those in any key, and to do them on these rudimentary synthesizers all from memory was a bit out of my skill set. He replaced me with the fabulous Bobby Martin.

Tony: I guess then, that's acceptable!

Lisa Popeil: He can play saxophone and had so much touring experience. I was funny. I was funny and I was cute. I did come out in my lingerie. I don't think Bobby did that!!

Tony: No, I don't think he did!

Lisa Popeil: We all have our special gifts. I'm glad that I got a call. It was probably in September from St. Louis. They were touring in St. Louis. Frank called me and said "You want to do this show at the Santa Monica Civic in December?" I said "Absolutely! What would you like me to do?" He said "Well, let's do that *Lisa's Life Story*" which was this semi-improvised thing we had thrown together. Then T*eenage Prostitute.* At the night of the show, he said "Let's do *Dangerous Kitchen*." I'd never done *Dangerous Kitchen*. He gave me the lyrics. It came out great because I did it in. what we call in the classical trade, the styles. I tried to sound like him. Then it turned into this wild improvisational thing where each musician would play something trying to stump me. It came out really great. I think everything's available somewhere, even though it may be in an edited form.

Some of the things like *Dangerous Kitchen* was recorded live at the show in December of '81. He took it back in the studio and he added things. He overdubbed some other tracks. It's much thicker and more rhythmic. I think *Teenage Prostitute* was definitely enhanced later in the studio. Then after that show, when he came back, he did have some things he wanted me to try. I went over it a few times. Some of it was, that he wanted me to do was very misogynistic. Yes. I didn't feel right about that. It didn't feel like a good fit for me.

Tony: Good for you, to be able to know that.

Lisa Popeil: Yes, I think it was *Spiders from Mars*. I think it was something like that. He had words for it. I always took issue with his view of women. They were more like tools or vessels.

Tony: Sure.

Lisa Popeil: Yet, he treated me with kindness and respect. He, in real life, I think, had great regard for women. For his wife and for his daughters. He was very egalitarian and respectful, but not in his music.

Tony: Right.

Lisa Popeil: I didn't want to be part of something that made women seem silly or stupid. I just didn't want to be made fun of or promote that for my own benefit somehow.

Tony: *The Dangerous Kitchen* came off of *Man from Utopia. Lisa's Life Story. You can't do that on Stage 6.*

Lisa Popeil: I thought *Dangerous Kitchen*, that's his version, right?

Tony: Yes, I believe so. that version you're talking about may not be available. I'm going to have to look. it might be. There's so much out there, and I know quite a bit, but this one's got me stumped. Somebody out there is yelling at us right now. It's available on this. Shaking their fist at us. Sorry, gang. There's a lot of bootlegs and stuff!

Lisa Popeil: Yes, right.

Tony: Yes. Pull out some bootleg and we'll find it.

Lisa Popeil: I have so many great photos. I just have so many wonderful photographic memories of that night.

Tony: Have you ever thought about publishing some of the pictures? I'm sure a lot of people would really like to see those.

Lisa Popeil: It's worth checking into if you think that there's the interest in them. There's ones with Ray White and Steve Vai backstage. Me and Frank backstage too.

Tony: Any pictures of any celebrity. There's a ton of people who are interested, especially ones that only exist only one place on the planet, and that's with you.

Lisa Popeil: Steve Vai and I were spending time together. I remember just hanging out with him at his apartment and playing music, and he came in for a couple of tracks on my album. I'm not sure which ones. I haven't been able to listen to that thing for a long time!

Tony: I can't listen to my old stuff either.

Lisa Popeil: If I were an actor, I'd probably be someone who can't watch any of my own movies.

Tony: Sure.

Lisa Popeil: I haven't stayed in touch with him as much as I'd like to over the years. I remember when we were both in our 20s, and he was super nice. He contacted me probably in the '90s, asking if I had the original 24-track tapes, because he wanted to go back into those songs that he'd recorded for me. I maybe transcribed the solos. I can't quite remember, but I didn't have the originals anymore. I hadn't kept them, so I wasn't able to give those to him.

Tony: That's too bad. That would have been interesting to see what he could do with those, years after the fact. Boy, that would have been something.

Lisa Popeil: That would have been very interesting.

Tony: You did a weird Al record, or at least one of his songs, Mr. Popeil. I think I remember hearing that.

Lisa Popeil: Mr. Popeil is based on Rock Lobster by The B-52s. I got a call from Al's manager, saying that they were going to record this song. It was a compilation of my dad and my brother and anyone else who'd ever sold gadgets on television. It was so surreal to go down to this audition. They were auditioning for the other female background vocalist. He wanted me to sing background vocals. I've recorded with Al on almost all his records. I get to see him every year or two. It's a great pleasure to see him and continue to work with him. I can't believe how prolific he's been. He just hasn't let up. He needs to be honored for his longevity.

Tony: It is amazing that he's been doing that type of music and doing it so well.

Lisa Popeil: Forever.

Tony: Who else has been doing that?

Lisa Popeil: Rolling Stones. Right. Rolling Stones. Who else has been consistently making records all this time? His shows are amazing. I'm considering doing an interview series, a video interview series of well-known pop and rock singers. He doesn't know it yet, but I'm going to hit him up because I think he'd be a great interview. His ability to go from screaming to soft and delicate and heartbreaking and have a totally healthy, clear voice at the end of a show, I don't know how he does it. it's not like we're kids anymore. We must be in the mid-50s now. He's all over the place. If any of your listeners have never seen the Weird Al show… you have to go! You won't believe what you're going to see. It's tight. The musicians have been all together. I know all the guys. The same guys from '83. They're on top of their game. Unbelievable musicians. To see a real bunch of musicians doing their thing is a thrill.

Tony: He's probably come to play near me here in Nashville.

Lisa Popeil: They're better now than they used to be. As good as they were, they're better now. They're not just sort of hanging out on their laurels. If you go to his website, I think they have a tour schedule. He usually tours in the spring and in the summer on the years that he does do it. He does a lot of state fairs too.

Tony: Do you get called by anyone like the *Ugly radio Rebellion* people. or any guys that are doing the Zappa cover band thing?

Lisa Popeil: No, I never have.

Tony: That would be interesting just because a lot of those guys go with them. Ike Willis for example. I've seen them a couple of times. That's really neat to see the actual players playing that stuff. I'm sure they'd love to have you!

Lisa Popeil: I'm open to it. I should go to Zappanale in Germany. Is that still going on?

Tony: I think so. There's actually a lot of things that are going on around the world regarding Zappa. I get over to Europe quite a bit, and I'd like to actually go see something like that while I'm over there,

Lisa Popeil: Yes, I think he's very popular in northern Europe still. He has his fans. On Facebook, I get a lot of people who write me to Facebook because they're Zappa fans, and that's always nice considering how many years it's been now. Has it been 30 years?

Tony: Yes.

Lisa Popeil: It's been over 30 years.

Tony: Isn't that hard to believe?

Lisa Popeil: That's because I haven't aged a bit.

Tony: No, me neither! I just get a bit more forgetful now!

Lisa Popeil: I hate that when that happens. That is why I couldn't go on tour. If you made any mistake at all, Frank would know not only that a mistake was made, but who made it. He'd glare at you. You get the hair stand up on the back of your neck. I'd think "I can't blow it. I can't blow it. I've got to cut it. What am I supposed to play next?"

Tony: I've heard the Buddy Rich horror stories where he would just kill you if you hit a wrong note. How did Frank handle the "off nights" with certain people? Were you just doomed, or did you were in trouble, but you didn't actually hear about it later?

Lisa Popeil: I know that he would glare, and I think I heard stories that if there was a piece being played and it fell apart, that he might humiliate you in front of the crowd, and then everybody starts over again. I don't think that was common though.

People would come and go. there weren't many players who played for more than a few years. I'm not really sure what the rationale for that was. I don't know why he would have auditions for the next tour and why he didn't keep people. I really don't know.

I had heard stories about how tough he was and merciless, and I saw some of that in the auditions. As much as I was struggling with our rehearsals because of the quantity of work and the impossibility of the work, meaning some of the work there were no fingerings for, I remember saying "Frank, I've played this section of this piece over and over, and I'm trying to find a good fingering for it, but there's no good fingering." I said "How did you write it?" He put up his two index fingers, and that said it all. What that told me was that when he wrote that passage, he did it with two fingers. He didn't play it like a pianist would play it, where they would sit underneath the fingers. There's unplayable passages, which are in famous works. I'd have these difficulties, and I'd get emotionally drained and feeling so frustrated with myself and doing the best I could.

At the end of a long day of rehearsal, he'd sit with me, and he was very fatherly and kind to me, and I thought that was unique. It didn't go with the picture that had been presented to me. It was very sweet and encouraging to me. I'll always remember that.

HOWARD KAYLAN

Howard Kaylan is a prominent American musician, singer, and songwriter, best known as the lead vocalist of the 1960s rock band The Turtles. Born on June 22, 1947, Kaylan, along with his musical partner Mark Volman, formed the core of The Turtles, a band that achieved considerable success with hits like "Happy Together," "Elenore," and "She'd Rather Be with Me."

Kaylan's distinctive voice and stage presence contributed significantly to The Turtles' sound and popularity during the mid-1960s. After The Turtles disbanded in the late 1960s, Kaylan and Volman joined Frank Zappa's band, the Mothers of Invention, adopting the stage names "Flo" and "Eddie" respectively. They continued to work with Zappa throughout the 1970s.

In addition to his work with The Turtles and Frank Zappa, Kaylan has had a diverse career in music. He has performed with various bands, collaborated with other artists, and released solo material.

Tony: On the line with me is a musician, an actor, a writer, a Turtle, and a Mother all at the same time. Who else could it be but Howard Kaylan? Howard, are you there?

Howard Kaylan: Hey, Tony, how are you, sir? Yes, I'm here!

Tony: Where are you at right now?

Howard Kaylan: I am in lovely Seattle, Washington. It's a great music city. It's a wonderful breakout town for bands particularly. Bands come here from all over the country thinking that they're going to make it and be the next Modest Mouse or Nirvana or

Pearl Jam or something, and most of them go away just empty-handed.

A lot of bands break out of here, and this is a great city for music. Maybe because it rains so much. Maybe because there's so much time spent indoors in clubs and stuff. The music is all pervasive here, and this is a very music town. You guys at Nashville, Music City USA, we're just sort of Grunge City USA.

Tony: Right. Everybody here is a songwriter, a country writer, because they all come here to try and make it big and buy a big mansion on the hill, which most of the time does not happen. I guess that's anywhere you go.

You've got a book out called *Shell Shocked: My Life with the Turtles, Flo and Eddie, and Frank Zappa*. Can you tell me a little bit about the book?

Howard Kaylan: I can tell you that the book is no-holes barred. I can tell you that it tells the entire truth and nothing but the truth, and that it's a shocker in a lot of ways, because I've had a most incredible career beginning in high school and taking me all the way to present day. I'm 66 years old now, so I've been doing nothing but being a Turtle or being a Mother all my life. This is what I do. I've never been a bricklayer. I don't know how to do anything else. I have no discernible talents whatsoever except for being able to do this. This is what I do proudly and gladly.

I always have loved it back in the high school days when you could graduate from school and four months later have a hit record on the charts and be on the road with the *Dick Clark Caravan of Stars* and having your parents go, "You were supposed to be in college!" I remember telling them "I'll go back to college if I don't have a hit record." Not just a record, but a hit record in the next six months. Within four months after making that stupid statement, fortunately we did have a hit record and it didn't stop.

The Turtles went on for about five and a half years of hit records. Then the Turtles broke up in a sea of lawsuits and litigation, and a record company blaming us for lack of sales. and us fining six and a half million dollars of misappropriated funds and taking them to court and winning. That suit taking so many years. During those years, my partner and myself couldn't call ourselves by our real names. We couldn't because of the lawsuit. All through the years, we were the Fluorescent Leech and Eddie.

Tony: Where did that come from? Who made that up?

Howard Kaylan: Frank said, listen, our lawyers are saying that you can't use your real names to be in this group. You got any other ideas? We knew we'd be in litigation and we had to come up with something. After racking our brains, we came up with the nicknames we had given two of our Turtle roadies way back in the day. One of them was very flamboyant and borrowed things and never gave them back. We always called him the Fluorescent Leech.

Tony: Nice!

Howard Kaylan: The other guy was very collegiate looking. Even though his name was Dennis Jones, we called him Eddie. He looked like an Eddie. The Fluorescent Leech and Eddie were our two roadies. When Frank heard that name, he laughed his ass off. That's when we knew it was going to work. Because our job in that band was not to make the audience laugh. Our job was to make Frank laugh.

Tony: I've heard that from several other people who played with him. I that's great!

Howard Kaylan: Absolutely. I'll tell you something... there was something about Mr. Zappa's laugh that was very infectious and very real. You knew that while he was working his audiences and even his employers, when it came down to the music, when it came down to being on stage, no one was more present or in the moment than Frank Zappa. He was the best on stage I have ever seen, ever.

Tony: You two guys were some of thee few members that were totally out front. Like doing *Billy the Mountain,* where it's actually like little plays. Especially where the music is really difficult AND you can also make it funny. It's perfect that you teamed up with a guy that wrote really hard to play music and also extremely funny stuff. What a combination!

Howard Kaylan: He was a very prophetic man. I'm not sure that I would have put us into that band back in 1970. It was a risky situation. Even the guys in his group at the first rehearsal were going. "Frank, are you sure? These are the Turtle guys. They've been on Ed Sullivan. Everybody knows these idiots. Are you sure you want to put them in your band? This is cutting edge stuff. We're supposed to be satire. These guys, don't do anything but hit records." It took them a while to see that Frank saw something else in us. He saw the comedy in the albums that we had put out, *Battle of the Bands* and things like that, where we had put ourselves into the identities of other bands and done an album of sort of satire. It wasn't mothers of invention satire. It was very light. It was us being just other bands and sort of doing songs tongue in cheek in that genre.

We had no illusions of trying to be the Mothers. We did not want to be that a comedy band. We just wanted to show that we could do more styles of music than just *Happy Together*. Frank had heard that in the grooves of the *Battle of the Bands* album where a lot of people hadn't. They questioned his judgment greatly. "Are you sure you're going to ruin your little jazz ensemble by putting in these two fat, funny guys from the world of pop music?" they would say. Frank knew exactly what he wanted to do. He knew that he wanted to step back out of the limelight for a minute, concentrate on writing more for orchestras, and play more guitar than he had in the past. In fact, he did, during our mothers of invention, play a lot more guitar. Sadly, when you listen to those records that we did, and the great ones were all live, just in a finale and the Fillmore album and all that, Frank took out his solos. He edited out all of his musical moments.

Tony: Really?

Howard Kaylan: The only places you can hear that stuff is on bootlegs. Otherwise, all the records that exist with the Fluorescent Leech and Eddie on them have been edited to death because Frank believed that it would be more valuable to have Mark and myself be a part of the record than just another solo. I think he was wrong. I think his instincts should have broken it up a little more evenly, and that perhaps the group that we were in wouldn't have been perceived as so much of a comedy band if Frank had let his guitar playing shine on those albums. He really didn't want to do that. He really wanted to be a second fiddle, so to speak, and let the band, for the first time, take over.

We were, as the Mothers, a real band. We went out on the road together. We rode in cars and planes and buses together. We hung out together before and after the shows. It was unlike any band that Frank Zappa had ever had before, and he was so immersed in it. We started writing together and going to dinner after the shows together and doing naughty things together... that you'll have to read about in my book! We really grew very close. By the time the group broke up because of, A: the fire in Switzerland that burned all our equipment, and, B: the incident at the Rainbow Theater where he got pushed off the stage. Between those two incidents, A: Frank wasn't able to tour for almost a year. B: he had people in his ear going, Look, Frank, the last thing you need is a band. You don't even know if you're going to be able to walk again. Let's just let these guys go. You'll put something else together in a year or so. It'll be great. No one will notice, and you'll continue on as usual, which I think Frank did pretty much.

He assembled a more jazz-oriented group and went on sort of not trying to be such a band, not trying to be such a pop group, but going back to his older days. But I loved that. I loved every phase of the Zappa existence. I think the best stuff he ever did, quite frankly, was the first stuff he ever did. That's me. I'm a fan. That was my first perception of the man was the genius of those first few records, and I still don't think anybody's come close to the satire that exists musically on those albums.

Tony: I think after you guys were gone, you guys did your Flo & Eddie album. You took Don Preston and Aynsley Dunbar and guys like that, and they were on that album too, right?

Howard Kaylan: Yes, it was the entire Mothers of Invention band that was on that album, because for an entire year, we did not hear from the Herb Cohen or Zappa's office about future plans. We didn't know Frank was going to even be in a band after he recovered.

Frank didn't know what he was going to do, and nobody told us anything. Nobody from the label, nobody from management, nobody from the Zappa office contacted anybody in the band for a year.

Now it's not just Mark and myself who don't have a job. It's everybody in the Mothers of Invention who doesn't have a job at this point in time. We're all trying to contact Frank to find out if there is ever going to be another tour or if there's going to be another Mothers of Invention or any answer.

In the interim, we're starving to death. Mark and I decided at this point, since we had no contractual obligations with Frank or anybody else at the time, since we had won our lawsuit against our record company as The Turtles, we had gotten our name back. We had earned all the masters back, and everybody else at The Turtles signed off. Nobody else in the band thought there was any future in owning those masters and signed off on them and just said, no, if you give me $1,000, I'll go away. We came up with the cash, and thanks to Alice Cooper and Shep Gordon, his manager, and bought out everybody else in the band and went to court for many years, Mark and I, and finally won the name back to The Turtles in about 1984 or so.

Then we started putting out albums all over the world because Mark and I wound up owning all of The Turtles' songs. That's the way we exist now. If you hear a Turtles' song in a commercial or in the motion picture or on the radio... that money goes to Mark and myself. We feel very fortunate that we had the foresight to know that there was going to be money up ahead for those recordings, to know that Happy Together and those songs were going to outlive us as a band, and to have the faith and confidence in the music that we had already made to put our money where our mouth was at the time and say, yes, we think these are worth something. We're going to pay to have the name Turtles for the rest of our lives. We did, and it has served us extremely well.

Tony: Now you guys weren't thrilled about the name Turtles when it first came around, were you?

Howard Kaylan: It's the stupidest name in the world. This was a name that our first manager, back in 1965 came up with because our original surf band name, The Crossfires, didn't seem like it was apropos to doing folk rock music. He came up with the name The Turtles, and we just rolled on the floor. We said "You've got to be kidding. That is the stupidest name we have ever heard in our lives. They're green, they're slow, they're slimy, they're fat, they're stupid. Why in the hell would we want to be Turtles?" He said "You're not looking at it the right way. There are so many English bands coming over now with animal names, and everybody is going to associate Turtles, Beatles, that T-L-E-S ending with a British group. You're coming out on a brand new label, and the Beatles were releasing things on Swan, on DJ, on Polly Records. You guys are going to be perceived as just another English band trying to break out of London."

He was absolutely right. For the first six months of our existence, everywhere we went, the posters said "Live from England, The Turtles." The early part of the touring, we didn't know how to react to it, so we all put on British accents. We talked to promoters like this, we asked them for white tea and Bangers and Mash and that sort of thing, and they complied. It was funny, but we didn't want to blow it. If they thought we were British, we didn't want to burst their balloons, so we were British for the first six months.

Then people got wise. Dick Clark had us on television a whole lot. Ed Sullivan had us on, and said we were from California. The bubble burst at that point. Just another band from L.A!

Tony: Just another band from L.A. I was thinking, like that Fillmore East album, where one side of the album, the payoff is Happy Together at the end. It's you guys trying to get chicks who only want to go with you IF they hear your big hit single in the chart... with a bullet. It's your REAL big hit single! I always thought "That's a brilliant idea!"

Howard Kaylan: Thank you. The genius of Frank Zappa. This is a story that I had told Frank one of the first days I was in the band. In fact, I was in San Antonio, Texas, and Frank and myself went across the street to a bar near the hotel. The name of the bar was Bwanna Dick.

Tony: You're kidding!

Howard Kaylan: I kid you not. That was the name of the bar. We laughed, and we remembered it, and we wrote it down. Then at that discourse that we were having at the table, Frank was asking me a whole bunch of stories about our past. If you listen to any album by the Mothers of Invention as a group, no matter who the players are, there's a lot of folklore in there. The stuff on the bus becomes the stuff of song.

Tony: Like when you join the Mothers, Frank was sort of renting you.

Howard Kaylan: Right. He owned your mind for as long as you were in that band, and anything you said, he could take credit for as a Mothers of Invention song. Not realizing that for the first few years of our existence with Frank, we told him everything that we ever knew.

One of the stories that I told Frank was the exact story as it appears on the White album, and as it concludes from that album and connects to 200 Motels. The story was, in a very brief sentence, that this was me. I did have a girl. She was in the room with me. It was a matter of "I love you, I love you, I love you, but I won't put out for you unless you sing me your big hit record with The Bullet!" I told this story to Frank, and Frank said "What did you do? What did you do?" I said "Frank, are you kidding? I sang it. I sang her my big hit record with The Bullet. What would you do?"

Tony: What else would you do?

Howard Kaylan: He laughed. He laughed and laughed and laughed and turned that into the story that became 200 Motels. The problem was that we ran out of time and money during the shooting of 200 Motels to shoot the ending of the picture. The ending of the picture was Mark in drag and me with the glitter in my beard as the pop star going to the nightclub in the tinsel car, as Frank called it, and doing the entire white album. "Do you like my new car? Yes, I do. It's a Fillmore, isn't it? Yes." All that stuff that follows. "Where are you staying?" and all of that groupie stuff, and "I am not a groupie, and sing me your hit record with The Bullet!!" That was supposed to be the ending of 200 Motels. It just never got filmed.

Tony: Never.

Howard Kaylan: It became the white album, and anybody who is curious as to how 200 Motels ends, all they have to do is listen to the white album. It was going to end with Happy Together.

Tony: I'll edit those two together for my collection becomes it's the correct way it should have been.

There's another thing. That movie, you're there with Ringo, and you had Keith Moon, and Theodore Bacall. that's some big people. I would think that no matter how big or popular you get, to hang out with Ringo or somebody like that is always going to be a little exciting or intimidating or something. What was that like?

Howard Kaylan: We had known him before. we had first met The Beatles in 1967 when The Turtles went over there on the strength of *She'd Rather Be With Me*. We had intimate contact with The Beatles that is chronicled pretty much in detail in both my book, *Shell Shocked*, and the movie, *My Dinner With Jimmy.*

It also talks about that very first meeting in London and how rude The Beatles were to us at the time, and how that later plays into the book and the movie and John Lennon and our whole situation with The Beatles and the way it was to follow in years' future.

In 1967, they were jerks to us. In later years, they became really friendly with us. It's hard to say exactly how I feel about The Beatles. I'm very ambivalent. I wouldn't be here without them. I'm smarter because I saw what they really were like.

Tony: You did background vocals and stuff with Bruce Springsteen, Alice Cooper, John Lennon, Duran Duran, and over a hundred different albums. You guys sang with everybody. That's amazing.

Howard Kaylan: It's true. I loved it. The fact is that if Mark and I were both living in the same city these days, we would probably still be doing background singing. It's very difficult to get the two of us together. The last people that pulled me out of Seattle and Mark out of Nashville to do any background singing were U2. We sang with them at Carnegie Hall a couple of years ago. That's pretty much it. We don't do a lot of vocalizing as a duo on records anymore because of our geographical differences.

We're out there every summer, June, July, and August every year with the Happy Together Tour. We tour all of North America. Those are the only touring dates basically that we do, those three months. It's intensive. We do go out on the road with four other acts and three buses and trucks and perform in all the major venues in America. For the past couple of years, we've been taking an entire busload of students from Nashville with us.

Tony: How exciting for them.

Howard Kaylan: It is. It's a great thing, and it's really good for us. Mark teaches at Belmont University, and he teaches music business. Every year the school has been generous enough to pitch in and supply a bus for these kids to travel along with us and learn the ropes of the road from the inside, how to be a tour manager, how to do lights, how to do sound, how to do promotion, how to do merchandising. They learn it backwards and forwards. When they leave that summer program, some of them have already made up their minds, no, this is not what I want to do at all. I thought I wanted music business. I do not want the music business. It's a pain in the butt.

Tony: At least they know.

Howard Kaylan: Yes, it is. Yes, they know from experience. They know from seeing guys who have been doing it for 30, 40 years at a time that this is going to be their life if they cheat.

Tony: I want to go! I'll just jump on the back of the bus and hold on. Hopefully no one will see me.

Howard Kaylan: You'll be safe. You'll be safe. We leave the first week in June, so get ready for a really long and intense summer.

Tony: I need to see you guys the next time around.

Howard Kaylan: A show like this, the Happy Together Tour, comes along once in a blue moon. You should see it because you don't know if it's ever going to happen again.

DON PRESTON

Don Preston is an American musician known primarily for his work as a keyboardist and composer. He is particularly renowned for his association with Frank Zappa and the Mothers of Invention, one of the most innovative and influential bands of the 1960s and 1970s.

Preston's involvement with Zappa began in the mid-1960s when he joined the Mothers of Invention as their keyboardist. His contributions to the band included playing a variety of keyboard instruments, including piano, organ, and synthesizer, as well as providing vocals and contributing to the band's avant-garde compositions.

Preston's keyboard skills and experimental approach to music were integral to the Mothers of Invention's sound, especially during their most prolific and groundbreaking period in the late 1960s and early 1970s. He played on several classic Zappa albums, including "Uncle Meat," "Hot Rats," and "Weasels Ripped My Flesh."

Tony: Hey Don, you're there?

Don Preston: Yep, I'm totally here! I'm on my new iPhone that I just got. Finally gave in and got one.

Tony: I'm f originally from Michigan, you're from up around Flint, aren't you?

Don Preston: I was born in Flint, but I grew up in Detroit.

Tony: I see. That's close. I started off over in Battle Creek, a little West of you.

Don Preston: I know Battle Creek. Cool little town!

Tony: Yes, but it's freezing cold up there in the winter, and I'm glad I'm not there now. Where do you live currently?

Don Preston:: I live in Los Angeles, and that's where I am.

Tony: I've seen you guys with *Grandmothers* and *Project Object*. Are you still out playing with anybody?

Don Preston: We've put together a new *Grandmothers of Invention* right now. We're still rehearsing. We're going to Europe at the end of this month and tour around there for a month, and then we have nine days off, and we're going to Australia and doing a bunch of touring there.

The band, well, one thing I have to say is that the lead singer, Napoleon, he decided to go in a different direction than us, so he's not with us now. On the other hand, Bunk Gardner rejoined this band, so now we have Bunk in the band.

Tony: Now, what did you guys do in the *Don and Bunk* show? I heard about it, but I never saw you guys.

Don Preston: We toured around the East Coast and Midwest as a duo, and afforded people the ability to hear some of the inner parts on various albums that they never probably couldn't hear as well as they could with just the two of us playing.

Tony: Right.

Don Preston: It was pretty successful. We did all of this material, the different Zappa's songs and everything, and played our parts the way we played them originally, and people loved it.

Tony: You put out you CD *Vile Foamy Ectoplasm.* In '93. Is that still available? Can people get that still?

Don Preston: Yes, you can. If you go to iTunes, I think you can find it there somewhere.

Tony: Very good.

Don Preston: Yes, it's still available. Actually, a different record company put it out maybe about eight years ago.

Tony: You did some of the synthesizer work on *Apocalypse Now*. That sounds interesting.

Don Preston: That was one of the more interesting things I've done in my life. They had three or four different guys working on the score, and I teamed up with Nyle Steiner, who was the inventor of an electronic saxophone type thing, and quite an amazing guy himself. He and I worked on about seven cues for the film, and my favorite was where Kurtz walks in and throws a severed head in this guy's lap. I had to watch that, about 80 times. It was even more realistic when I was watching it than in the movie. I've done about 20 other feature films as well. Don't miss out on *Blood Diner*!

Tony: Sounds great. Blood Diner.

Don Preston: You may hate me for recommending that one!

Tony: Speaking of movies, of course, you've got *200 Motels*, and then you've got *Uncle Meat*. I'll try not to make you mad... or you'll turn into The Monster! How funny is that?

Don Preston: Yes, most people like that.

Tony: Who came up with that? Was it you? Was it Frank?

Don Preston: I have a picture when I was, 21, me and my sister. We're sitting together on a couch, and both of us are holding horror magazines. We actually made a movie together where there's a giant fly and a Dracula character, and all kinds of goodies like that. and a castle that burns down and everything.

Tony: Cool!

Don Preston: It was, quite an industrious project. The only thing is we couldn't afford a sound camera, so we had this really nice camera that doesn't have sound. We solved that problem by, holding up balloons that said what we were saying… like a cartoon!

Tony: Wow!

Don Preston: That worked.

Tony: What was that, like in the 60s?

Don Preston: Ye did that movie, around 69, I think.

Tony: A lot of movies in the 60s did that, film them with no sound at all and put it in later. Some people did a better job than others of overdubbing the sound.

Don Preston: I did add music to the film and sound effects, so that's all there too.

Tony: The beauty of that today is you just do it on your computer. it's so easy for things like that to be done. It is a whole new world as far as what people can do creatively. I talk to a lot of people, and they all have a laptop, and they've got a big recording studio right in front of them at the house, where before, you had to go and spend thousands of dollars... and now it's just right at home. Boy, how convenient.

Don Preston: It is. It's amazing. I went over to a friend's house the other day that he and I – well, I did a bunch of films in the studio that he and I worked in, and we exclusively used the

Synclavier for all of those films. He's still doing that, but the Synclavier is sitting over in a corner, like all packed up, and they never use it anymore.

Tony: Not anymore.

Don Preston: It's amazing.

Tony: That was the first one. when it came to sampling and things like that was it. Of course, it $100,000 when it came out or something like that?

Don Preston: Yes, somewhere around that.

Tony: When it came out, it was out of most people's reach, but then, like everything else, they figured out how to make it smaller and cheaper. Let me ask you, I know you were friends with Bob Moog, which that just in itself has got to be interesting as far as the creation of analog synthesizers and things like that, and I've always been a big fan of the analog synthesizer, which, virtually went away... and now is making a comeback. Are you a fan the new type synths, or do prefer the old analog ones?

Don Preston: Let's put it this way. I always bring a mini-Moog with me when I tour.

Tony: Right.

Don Preston: No matter where I am, I always have a mini-Moog. That's a mini version of the old modular synths, which I had at one point.

Tony: There's a company called Native Instruments that I use a lot that has gone out and done an amazing job of finding all these old analog synthesizers and sampling and recording them. Things that you haven't heard in decades, and they found them and recorded them, and not just recorded the sound but recorded just all kinds of nuances.

For the person that really would like to have a collection old synthesizers, which you can only find in a museum nowadays, you can find a really good copy of it that you can use from your computer. All the oscillators and everything that was there has been recreated. That's loads of fun because you're bringing back a time that doesn't exist anymore. I've got a whole collection of those, and it's just – I just like knobs and buttons.

Don Preston: I like knobs too, but the problem with those synthesizers, it's very hard to turn a knob on your computer screen. If you're performing live, that's not something you want to do. I prefer a real knob to a virtual knob any day.

Tony: The only advantage that I ever saw you could tweak all those knobs to get a certain sound, and then it saves it to memory for using later!

Don Preston: You're right. I have an Arturia Minimoog, and they also make modular Moogs. All you need is a controller that has a whole bunch of knobs on it.

Speaker 2: Yes, right.

Don Preston: You can assign all those knobs to all the knobs on the screen.

Tony: I remember when they came out with the presets for synthesizers.

Don Preston: The Prophet 5 is one of the first ones to have memory and store whatever sounds you came up with, I think. I will say this, if you're fooling with a modular Moog or even a Minimoog, it's true, you can't change sounds as easily as you can on a sampler. A sampler can never do what a modular Moog does, like in terms of electronic music.

Tony: Sure, of course.

Don Preston: That's the main reason I got involved with these in the first place, is to be able to do electronic music.

Tony: Do you have any other keyboards that you really like? that you have kept around or have gone out and found that are a little bit older but are classics?

Don Preston: Not really. these things wear out. Of course, I had a Minimoog when they came out, but that thing got to the point where it was unplayable. Nowadays I use things like Chaos Pad and the Air Synth, which you wave your hand over it and it's like a theremin, but it has all these unbelievable sounds in it that you can create. you can manipulate with your hands waving around.

Tony: How did you meet up with Zappa and the gang and start a band? How did that come about?

Don Preston: I met Zappa at a concert that he and I were playing at. There were like five stages. We were both in the center stage, in the middle of the entire giant room. We started talking, we gave each other cards and stuff, and I got a call from him about three weeks later wanting me to play with him at a place, an audition, a place called Bank Club in Anaheim or something like that.

We went there and played No in 7/4, which caused a lot of people problems when they tried to dance to it. Of course we didn't get the gig. Then Zappa started coming over to my house and we had jam sessions there with Bunk and Buzz Gardner and a few other people that you probably don't know. We wound up playing an audition at ABC because I think Zappa's father worked there at the time.

Tony: I see.

Don Preston: It was very strange because we set up all our stuff. We weird gongs and brackets from a railroad that holds down the rails. You can play them, they're tuned differently. I had a leaf springs from a truck that we also set up like a vibraphone. All kinds of junk like that.

Then we saw all these heads peeking around the corner. They were the musicians that worked there. They couldn't believe their eyes. "What in the hell were they going to do?" Of course I had the bicycle with me.

Tony: Yes, of course. The famous bicycle that was on The Tonight Show. The Steve Allen Show.

Don Preston: Yes, right. Anyhow, we played and we didn't get that gig either! It was fun. Then about two years later Zappa showed up at my tour.\

I had never seen him look like what we know Zappa looks like. All the time prior to this it looked like his high school graduation picture. Short hair and everything and very astute looking. Now he showed up at my doorstep with his long hair and he had a monkey coat on that looked like his hair. I didn't know who this guy was. Finally he told me who he was. Then I said "My God. what happened to you?"

He would come over from time to time and mostly was interested in talking to my now ex-wife because she had all kinds of ideas like *Take your clothes off when you dance* and everyone should be free. and all that. Right. Sort of the beginnings of hippie consciousness.

Tony: Right, sure.

Don Preston: Anyhow, that's how that all started.

Tony: You guys at some point just said *The Mothers* was going to be the name of the band?

Don Preston: Actually, they wouldn't print *The Mothers* in the newspaper.

Tony: Yes.

Don Preston: Because it indicated something else.

Tony: Yes, right, sure.

Don Preston: Which I won't say. Actually it was Tom Wilson who was our liaison to MGM Records. I think he did or somebody that thought up the name *The Mothers of Invention* and that stayed with us.

Tony: Another Zappa thing that I wanted to get into a little bit is the film *200 Motels*. I've seen that thing over and over trying to make sense of it, and it's just hilarious. I was talking to Howard Kaylan. Howard said "The Beatles weren't nice to us at first." Did you ever say to yourself, "Wow, that's Ringo from The Beatles. This is really cool!" What was your feeling on some of those guys being around there?

Don Preston: At that particular time I hadn't met any of the other Beatles. When there's all this time you have to wait in between shots. And they're setting up something new. we would just go over and jam. The drums were all set up and there was a keyboard there and a couple of the other guys, the bass player and everything. I have a story about the bass player. I can't think of his name right now. The guy that was playing bass with the Mothers at that time. There's a whole scene in the movie where he's stealing all this stuff out of the room.

Tony: Right.

Don Preston: He was so afraid that people would think that he stole stuff out of rooms that he quit the film. He walked out. We're all sitting around in the dressing room saying "Well, who are we going to get?" The first guy we tried out was the guy who was, I think he was Ringo's uncle.

Tony: A driver or something like that.

Don Preston: No, no. I'm saying that the first guy we tried out. He was about 65 years old. At one point, he had to say all these curse words and everything. He turned to Frank and he said, I just can't do this. I just can't.

Tony: There goes another bass player.

Don Preston: He quit.

Tony: Number two down the drain, okay.

Don Preston: Then we're sitting in the dressing room again and Ringo's driver comes in. He opens the door and says "Anybody want anything? I'm going to go into town and get some stuff." It turned out that he played bass. It was almost like, "Grab him. Yes, you're it. He's a good-looking guy. He's very charismatic." He did the part.

Tony: I bet he didn't see that coming.

Don Preston: No. Martin Lickert was his name.

Tony: That's just amazing. Being at the right place at the right time, I guess, always counts. Really?

Don Preston: No kidding.

Tony: The synthesizer that you built.... Is that long gone. or is that in the basement somewhere?

Don Preston: No, I think I dismantled it at some point. It was unique. there was nothing like it. I put together a whole bunch of oscillators and filters and ways of triggering them. I had a theremin built into the box, among other things. It was really good. It was a great tool to do that music, which was called upon in *The Mothers* even every so often.

Tony: Now, it didn't look like something you could just lug around, though. It looked like it was pretty stationary.

Don Preston: Not really. It wasn't that big. It was like about three feet by two feet by two feet. I think that's the dimension of it. It had a handle on top. You could carry it around.

Tony: Building your own keyboards! It's just not done anymore by people at home. That's what makes that stuff so fascinating to me. It's like, back in those days, that's what you had to do.

Don Preston: You couldn't buy anything. That was the problem. I found that there was no such thing, available as a unit. Then it was only like months maybe later that Moog came out with his synthesizer..

Tony: Did you ever check with anybody to see if they wanted to mass produce your invention?

Don Preston: No. I was only interested in what it could do for me.

Tony: Did you give it a name?

Don Preston: *My Electronic Box*, that's what it was called!

Tony: Who do you recommend people listen to? You've got your John Cage and you've got people like that. Do you have a short list of people that you really like in the electronic music field?

Don Preston: One of my favorites, Ligeti. Yes. He did some of the music in 2001.

Tony: How about recording? It must be fantastic to have literally hundreds of tracks to work with in the studio compared to what you had in the 60's.

Don Preston: We were experimenting with trying to get more and more tracks. I think we had a five-track happening then.

Tony: Now people couldn't imagine recording anything with only four tracks.

Don Preston: You can't even get the drums on that. No. That's crazy talk.

Tony: I know. I see you did something with John Lennon. What did you do with him?

Don Preston: It's not actually what I did with him. It's what he did with us.

Tony: Okay, then. Even better!

Don Preston: Frank gave me a call, and they were playing at the Filmore East, and he asked me to come down and sit in. I had a Mini Moog then, so I hauled that down to the show and set it up. During the middle of the concert, John and Yoko came out on stage.

They proceeded to do stuff with the band. At one point, Yoko got in this burlap bag, and everybody was chanting, scumbag. Then I played a pretty long electronic music solo.

Tony: Did The mothers ever do anything with film scoring?

Don Preston: The Mothers did a live track for a movie. It was *Ride for Your Life* or something like that. It was about a motorcycle.

Tony: That one I hadn't heard of. I'm going to have to do research on that.

Don Preston: We did it in Montreal at the Canadian Film Center or something like that.

Tony: Was it to music or were you making it up as you went? \ Who did that?

Don Preston: We made it up as we went, with Zappa with his hand signals and the way we could improvise and all that. It was just made up, I'm sure. We didn't play any compositions, that I remember. You can probably find it on YouTube. I don't know.

Tony: There's a recording of *The Don Preston Story*. What is it?

Don Preston: Okay, this guy came from Norway. He had already done a big, huge bio of Jimmy Carl Black, and I think he's already done one with Arthur Barrow, and he wanted to do one with Bunk and myself.

His name was John Larson**,** and he came here to California, and we all met in Arthur Barrow's studio. Then they interviewed us one at a time, and we went through our entire life story. It wound up being on two CDs. We were in tears at certain points. It was just really heavy. Then they put in all this weird sound effects to it.

Tony: Well, all good interviews need the weird sound effects!

Don Preston: Actually, I did a whole electronic music album for John as well. It's called *Colliding Galaxies*.

Tony: Did you record that here, or did you go over to Norway or someplace to record it?

Don Preston: No. I recorded it in my studio here.

Tony: Was that all done on the synthesizer you built, or on different things?

Don Preston: No, it was all different. The first one was, of course, before they had synthesizers, so that was done on the one I had, plus, the Fender Rhodes. I had an RMI piano as well, and I was putting that all through an Echo Plex I had.

Then the second one was done with a modular Moog, and the Mini-Moog, and a few other little toys I had. The third one was done with that same configuration, but added a percussionist onto it.

Tony: A live percussionist? Did he overdub later, or was he with you at the time?

Don Preston: No, we did it together.

Tony: Was this all something that you could reproduce live, let's say, later on?

Don Preston: In the case with electronic music, you can reproduce the tone of what you were doing.

Tony: Right.

Don Preston: I don't mean a specific tone, but the characteristics of that segment, whereas it wouldn't be the exact same thing. In other words, there's no music or anything, you're just going from one thing to another, and each thing leads into a different thing. You're constantly switching patches and all that.

Tony: Cool. I have a lot of that stuff here in my studio. I can sit here and twirl knobs by the hour and just sit back and go listen to how it sounds. It's so creative. It's not like writing a song with lyrics and a verse and chorus. It's amazing what's coming back... things with knobs all over them.

Don Preston: It hasn't all gone away.

BOBBY MARTIN

Bobby Martin is an American musician, songwriter, arranger, and producer best known for his work in the realms of soul, R&B, and funk music. He was highly regarded for his talents as a multi-instrumentalist, vocalist, and music arranger.

Martin's career spanned several decades, during which he collaborated with numerous prominent artists and bands. He gained widespread recognition for his work with Philadelphia International Records, where he served as a key arranger and producer. Martin contributed to the success of many hits released by Philadelphia International, including songs by artists such as The O'Jays, Harold Melvin & the Blue Notes, and Billy Paul.

One of Martin's most notable collaborations was with the legendary soul group, The Stylistics. He worked closely with them, arranging and producing many of their songs, helping to shape their signature sound.

Tony: It's Bobby Martin!

Bobby Martin: Hey Tony, how are you doing?

Tony: Pretty good! You're in Los Angeles aren't you?

Bobby Martin: I am, I am. It's a beautiful sunny day here.

Tony: I did a little bit of research. and of course. we all know you played with Frank. and that is the idea of this show. I just made a list of people you've performed, or recorded with... Paul

McCartney, Michael McDonald, Stevie Nicks, Kenny Loggins, Prince, Michael Bolton. You've been around!

Bobby Martin: It's been quite a ride and it ain't over yet and I'm just loving every minute of it and have been for many, not years but decades.

Tony: What are you doing with most of those guys?

Bobby Martin: In most of those situations they would generally try to take advantage of everything I do. I did get to whip out all kinds of different instruments, and sing along, and that's been great because I can't say that I love any one more than any other and I wouldn't want to give any one of them up.

That's why I did not go into just the classical thing. I just couldn't put on the blinders and say, okay, I'm going to be a symphony French Horn player for the rest of my life. There were too many other kinds of music I loved and too many other things I loved ways of expressing that I love to do with saxophone and singing and keys and everything.

Tony: That seems to be a theme with everybody I talk to. If you do one only thing, you can starve to death. You've got to branch out and do whatever you can for whoever you can.

Bobby Martin: Unless you're Steve Vai.

Tony: Yes, that's true. I don't see him playing the banjo very much.

Bobby Martin: I'd like to see him try though! I bet he'll do that when he gets 70 or something. He'll probably put out a banjo album.

Tony: Now you're in *Band From Utopia*. You guys play Frank's songs all over the place.

Bobby Martin: Yes, now that's a new thing, a new focus and it's been really great. We were contacted by the promoters of the *Jazz Open Festival* in the summer of '94, six months after Frank died. They asked us if we would put together a band of alumni to honor Frank's life in music and do some shows over there. We did and it was amazing. It was a pretty emotional experience because his loss was very fresh. We managed to handle that and just had such a great time doing it that we decided to keep doing it.

For the next few years, we did shows with various different lineups because different ones of us were available at different times. *Band From Utopia* was a viable entity for a couple of years there, but then it all just disappeared, just petered out as we all went on to other things.

Then the way it came back together again was two years ago in 2012, I was over performing at the *Zappanale Festival* in Germany and a couple of guys from Norway, who have become good friends, approached me about headlining a Zappa festival that they had planned for that fall of 2012. I said "Sure, that would be great fun. Let's do it." I performed there and headlined that festival with a great band from Norway. It went really well. They said "Wow, this was great. Can we do this again? Please come back with a band of Zappa alumni. That would so rock if we could do that." I said "Yes, great idea." I started contacting the guys and we basically put back together a band of alumni, basically reformed yet another iteration of a *Band From Utopia* and headlined the *Zappa Union Festival* in Oslo this past November. Everybody just had a ball. We're loving doing it.

We did a tour actually following that for a couple of weeks throughout five countries in Europe in November. We're gearing up to do another one towards the end of March and beginning of

April. I'm doing a couple of concerts in Holland in March, the 22nd and 23rd. Then the rest of the band is going to come over and we're going to do a couple more weeks. Everybody's loving doing it. The fans are loving it. The response from all over the world has been amazing.

We even had one guy come all the way from Japan to Oslo for the *Zappa Union Festival* that we just did in November. It's been great. It's been really fun to do, enjoyable to do. Again, one of the aspects of playing with Frank that I always loved has come back into my life again, which is getting to play not just that great music with Frank back in those days, but getting to play it with amazing musicians. These guys are just ridiculously brilliant and it's just wonderful fun to be on stage doing this with them again.

Tony: Were you a Zappa fan before you got into Frank's band?

Bobby Martin: I was very much aware of Frank, Actually. I was a senior in high school in '66 when Freak Out came out. I was aware of Frank right from the beginning. I was really pretty blown away by that album. It was so different and fresh and new and innovative.

When he came to Philly the following year in '67, I went to see him at the Spectrum in Philadelphia. It was a great show, an amazing show. Then seven years later, I went to see him again at the Spectrum again. That was in '74, which was a great band with George Duke and Nappy and Tom and Chester and Ruth. That was a brilliant show. I was, again, pretty flabbergasted by how far he had gone in the seven years since I'd seen him previously. Then seven years after that, in '81, I joined the band.

Tony: Who was the drummer then when you joined?

Bobby Martin: It was Chad. Chad came in the same year as me. '81.

Tony: All right. I thought so.

Bobby Martin: All the tours that I did with Frank, Chad was the drummer.

Tony: I talked to Lisa Popeil, who got hired for like, a week to do keyboard.

Bobby Martin: Right, I know. I was there.

Tony: She's said "I was replaced by Bobby Martin!" Or is it Robert? See, I want to say Bobby, because I've known you as Bobby Martin for years.

Bobby Martin: That's okay! I have a Bobby Martin Facebook page!

Tony: Okay, all right.

Bobby Martin: It's okay.

Tony: Lisa didn't feel too band about being replaced by YOU! It wasn't like ME that replaced her! t was somebody that can really play! It could have been like "Get out, and Tony's going to replace you!" That would have been just humiliating,

Bobby Martin: Yes, come on. Don't downgrade yourself like that.

Tony: Hey, my left hand sucks. My right hand's pretty good, but my left hand is always dumb. Maybe if I get a scale book and just sit there by the hour and just play scales, it might get a little better, but I started out on the accordion!

Bobby Martin: Do you play the Godfather theme?

Tony: See, back in the day. it used to be a classical instrument. They used to play cool European things, and then all of a sudden they started making Billy Joel and Elton John arrangements for the accordion. It became a joke, because those are horrible to listen to on that instrument.

Bobby Martin: There were some pretty darn good players though.

Tony: There are instruments that are made for certain styles of music, and you just shouldn't make them cross over into other things.

Bobby Martin: The accordion and its variations, various French squeeze box items have really come back into vogue through the whole Cajun New Orleans thing. It's become sort of cool and hip again.

Tony: You've got those MIDI accordions now, where you can sound like any instrument you want. I talked to Ed Mann, who uses the MIDI MalletCat, and it can sound like anything.

Bobby Martin: You could have a revival. You could join a Zydeco band and revive your accordion career.

Tony: One hing that really stands out that you did, is when you sang *Whipping Post* with Frank. How did you get assigned to sing that one?

Bobby Martin: I already knew that song. I met the Allman Brothers in '71. I was down at the South Jersey Shore. That was my first summer after leaving school, and I met this guy from Nashville that went to military school with Greg when he was 14 or something. When they played at the Steel Pier in Atlantic City, I went to see him and hung out with him backstage. I was aware of them, and I knew that song.\

85

In that band, we used to do Allman Brothers. It was a kick-butt band that I had in '71. We had a front man that did the song, and it always frustrated me because I thought "Man, I would love to do this song." Then a couple years later, I was in a different band, and I did get to sing it. I had known it for a long time. I'd known it since the '70s.

When Frank, just out of the blue one day in rehearsals for the first tour, said "Do you know *Whipping Post*? I said "Whoa, do I know Whipping Post? You bet!" He said "Okay, great. Teach it to the band, have it ready for rehearsal tomorrow." I did, and we did it, and it became the show-closing encore. It was just immense fun for me. a different thing for Frank because he wasn't into covering other people's material too much. Yes, it became an iconic rendition, and it was just immense fun. My one complaint was that he always played it too darn fast.

Tony: It's a cool song, and it's not just a straight four. It's got some pretty cool time things happening there. it's just weird enough that it fit.

Bobby Martin: Yes, it had the intro at 11, and then went to 12 for the rest of the song. Yes.

Tony: Now, speaking of weird time things, were you comfortable with all that crazy things that Frank threw at you? Some people could handle it, and some had to really fight to feel it.

Bobby Martin: Again, I had intensive classical training. When I first went through the audition process and all that, I was able to sight-read these crazy, complex things. I don't know, maybe it comes second nature to people more so than, some people more so than others. It was never really that much of a stretch for me.

I remember when Brubeck came out with the *Take Five* record, and that was like, whoa, this is really cool. When you look at it, the stuff Frank was doing was so far beyond that. It made Brubeck's record look like kindergarten. When you look at the blazing fast seven in Inca Roads, for instance, when George did the keyboard solos. Now, we do that too, but we actually separate the keyboards up into trays between saxophone and guitar. We like to try and switch things up a little bit. Ed takes the first solo in that song on mallets. We like to do things that are a little bit surprising, but very effective at the same time.

Different cultures throughout the world have sort of different approaches to not only time, but pitch. There are microtonal scales that are common, and people grow up with them. It's normal for a baby in Romania to hear, 14 or 16 tones of the scale and odd time signatures. It's just whatever you grew up with. It's not like humans aren't capable of it. If you're not comfortable with it, then you need to do whatever you have to do.

Set up a loop in 11 and just get comfortable playing over it and shed with it on your own if that's what you need to do. Yes, that was something that we had to do. We also had to do not only odd time signatures 7 and 5 and 11 and all that stuff, but we had to learn to do tuplets accurately over another signature. For instance, at the end of Black Page, there are 3 bars in a row where it's 11 over a 4/4 measure. A series of 11 tuplets for 3 bars in a row. Frank would just have us play that and cycle it over like a reggae groove and play 2 bars of reggae and then do the 11s and then 2 bars of reggae and then do the 11s until it was comfortable and smooth and we felt it and it was natural. Repetition is the mother of skill. Necessity is the mother of invention. Repetition will get you there. That's what we did as a group. If you needed to do more on your own, then you take it upon yourself and be responsible and do it on your own too.

Tony: I had heard that Frank would actually write out things that appeared to be scales and would say, here, take this home and play this scale and magically that group of notes became something that was a song he was working on. Did you ever get that? Where it's like you just thought, I'm just practicing this to practice it, but it actually became something.

Bobby Martin: Yes, that did happen. In fact, he would sometimes write out on a, just on some music paper, a tone row, an arbitrary tone row that he would create and say, okay, here are the notes that are allowed and we're going to improvise using these notes, using this tone series. He would also do things like that in terms of chords. Here's how you are going to structure this chord and that's what we're going to improvise over. Yes, sometimes it did turn into something.

That was one of the great things about working with Frank too. Things constantly changed and evolved and grew and he was very much into spontaneity and creativity. That was, rather than the exception, that was the rule, that was the norm. That was great for your brain, great for your fingers, great for your psyche and everything to be in that spontaneous creative atmosphere.

Tony: Now I know that Lisa Popeil was saying that she had some passage and she asked Frank "You don't have any fingering on this. How did you play it?" Frank's just like "Well, I just pounded it out with one finger. You figure out the fingering. That's your problem."

Bobby Martin: Yes, figure it out. That reminds me of a very funny story and I heard an interview with Tommy Mars and I remember distinctly going through this with Tommy in rehearsal. There's a passage in *Jumbo Go Away,* where it's just ridiculously impossible keyboard part and, Tommy was struggling with it and struggling with it. Tommy's brilliant. He's got blazing technique and this was like a real challenge for him. Frank was just watching him try to figure it out and smiling and Frank said "You want me to come up there and play it?": Tommy says "Come on, Frank, be serious. I'm trying to work this out." because, Tommy figured, well, if he's having this much trouble, there's no way in hell Frank as a guitar player can play this. Frank came up and he just whipped it right out.

The thing was. when he wrote it, he conceived it as a two-handed piece. When he showed Tommy how he arranged his hands over the keyboard and worked it out with the two hands, It was simple. It was kindergarten simple. Trying to do it with one hand was just virtually impossible.

As a keyboard player, you look at this passage in one restricted area of pitches and you figure "Okay, well, it's one restricted area. I'm going to do it with one hand. I'm going to actually use two hands and stack them one over the other and, assign certain notes to the left hand and certain notes to the right." It became ridiculously easy and sounded fabulously incredible because it was just, it sounded way more difficult than it was if you actually did the fingering the way Frank conceived it. That was a very interesting aspect of it, too.

Tony: Do you think or could you relate what Frank did, which was always a little different, but was it based on any other culture's music, or something that's similar?

Bobby Martin: Other culture? I wouldn't really say any other culture. I would say it was an amazingly eclectic mix of various,

American styles of music. Everything from jazz to doo-wop to classical and modern new music classical, heavy metal rock.

We had to be able to play all of those things with total authenticity and change on a dime from one to the next, depending on whatever hand signal he might give us, where something that was, at the moment, heavy metal would turn into Mr. Rogers style and then go into reggae and then go into country, and we had to do all that. I would say it was just an amazing amalgam of a broad cross-section of lots of American music.

Tony: I remember Ed was telling me he had a lot of freedom to try things with Frank. Like he'd say "I'll try xylophone on this part." Did you guys have that freedom to choose what sounds you wanted, or what instrument to play on a particular piece?

Bobby Martin: It was a case-by-case basis, but Frank was very open to all kinds of possibilities, and he would take a suggestion, and if that didn't work, he would know it right away, and if he had another idea, he would suggest that, or if he didn't, he'd say "What do you think?" or "What sound do you think it ought to be?" and so that was a fun aspect of it as well, and a perfect example of the sonic palette and his approach to this whole thing.\

Unlike a lot of other situations where you were, as a basically quote-unquote side man, you were under the thumb of the primary artist, and they tried to use whatever you could do to enhance their show and what they wanted to present, but you were pretty restricted in a lot of the situations that I worked in, but with Frank, it was exactly the opposite. He would put you. instead of under the thumb, he would put you under the microscope and find out every possible sound you could create in any way, whether it was a mouth noise, a body noise, an instrument of any kind, and he would figure out a way to use that to his advantage and make interesting, wonderful music with it.

A perfect example, we were in Zurich, Switzerland, on the '82 Tour, and I always liked to get up early and go out and explore, because these were places I'd never been before, so it was fascinating to me, and so I went out and I found this little shop where this little old man made Alcorns horns. The big, long, wooden ones. The Ricola thing!

Tony: Ricola, right, sure, yes.

Bobby Martin: I bought two of those and brought them back to the hotel, and the longer one of the two was so long that the tiny hotel room could not contain it, and so I hung the end of it out the little balcony and was playing it, and I wasn't aware of it at the time, but Frank was outside, downstairs, having lunch at the outdoor cafe, and he heard this and realized pretty quickly that it was me, and told me, bring those, I want them in the show tonight.

Of course. The Alcorns were in the show that night, and me and Tommy Morris did sort of trade back and forth with this wonderful sort of French horn sound he would create on one of his analog Moog synths, so that was a perfect example of Frank's spontaneity and wanting to just use everything his musicians could possibly do. He was very much into exploring the capabilities of all these wildly innovative musicians that he worked with over the years.

Tony: A lot of times you guys had samples of dogs barking and just all kinds of stuff. Who was in control of those samples?

Bobby Martin: That would vary. On the '88 tour, he brought his Synclavier out. and that was a time when sampling technology had really come a long way, and sometimes he would actually trigger it. but we also had it set up so that I could trigger it sometimes too. I think, as I recall, Ed could even trigger it from some MIDI controllers that he had as well.

Another thing that reminds me of one of my funniest Zappa memories was on the '88 tour We did some jazz-spoof things. In fact, one of the records, one of the double CDs from that tour is called *Make a Jazz Noise Here.* We used to goof on the sounds that some jazz musicians tend to make when they're playing, and these funny grunts and groans and things. Walt Fowler made some, recorded some sounds into Ed's sampling gear, and Ed would then trigger them with a MIDI-controlled pad. At one point, he got the idea "Hey, I can pitch-shift these things with a pedal controller." He took one of these sounds that Walt had made and pitch-shifted it, right while Frank was in the middle of drinking some coffee. Frank just totally broke up with wild laughter and spewed coffee out his nose and all over the place. It was just hilarious. The sound that Ed made with the sample was hilarious, and Frank's response was classic.

Tony: You hear them all the time. I bought this weird tube thing that got used a lot for crazy sounds. You turn it upside down and it sorta honks and squeaks, I picked it up at a gas station and went "Hey, there's that weird instrument thing Frank sampled!"

Bobby Martin: Right. You swing it around, and the air column, depending on how fast you swing it, you can shift it from the fundamental to the first harmonic to the second harmonic.

Tony: I don't even know what you call it, but I like it. You can buy it for a dollar, and they're loads of fun.

ARTHUR BARROW

Arthur Barrow is an American musician known for his work as a bassist, keyboardist, and composer. He is particularly recognized for his association with Frank Zappa, the iconic composer, musician, and bandleader.

Barrow's collaboration with Zappa began in the late 1970s when he joined Zappa's band as a bassist and keyboardist. He played on several of Zappa's albums during this time, including "Joe's Garage," "Tinsel Town Rebellion," and "You Are What You Is." Barrow's versatile musicianship and ability to handle complex compositions contributed significantly to Zappa's music during this period.

In addition to his work with Zappa, Barrow has pursued a diverse career in music. He has performed and recorded with numerous artists across various genres, including Robby Krieger of The Doors, Diana Ross, and Janet Jackson, among others. He continues to be admired by fans and respected by fellow musicians for his skillful playing, creative approach to music, and dedication to his craft.

Arthur Barrow: Hey Tony. How are you doing?

Tony: I'm good! You've worked with all kinds of people! I made a little list... Billy Idol, Janet Jackson, Keith Emerson, the Motels, Diana Ross, Joe Cocker. I had to stop because I got tired of writing!

Arthur Barrow: It's all true.

Tony: You have a big Doors connection, one of my favorites right there! How did you get in with Robbie Krieger?

Arthur Barrow: That spans from when I first moved out here till just the day before yesterday when we did a show, but I had met Don Preston on a Top 40 gig, and Don knew Robbie and was playing in Robbie's band at the time, and they rehearsed over at Don's place. I don't think Robbie realized I was a musician because we had a studio over there at Don's, and I was engineering stuff, and Robbie asked me if I would mix sound for them at the Whiskey. They were going to do a show there, and so I did.

I think that's the one and only time I've ever mixed live sound in my life. I just got to know him a little bit then, and then shortly after, I guess it was before Frank, I got a call from him about doing some synthesizer work. This was like early, this was '77 or maybe '78. I had some synthesizer gear, some early analog stuff and they were working on their American Prayer album. I don't know if you're familiar with that, but that's the one where they had a bunch of poetry of Jim Morrison's recorded by Jim, and then they put music behind it, and so they'd done it all, and I thought it was actually a fairly successful effort.

They had one track that was called The Movie that they wanted some eerie synthesizer sounds on, and so that's what I worked on.

It's interesting the way things worked out over the years. I just made some eerie noises, and Morrison says "Welcome to the theater." or something. "The movie will begin in five moments." and at one point he says "Did you have a good life when you died?" Enough to base a movie on.

It's basically, the first thing you hear is my little synthesizer, and you go, ooh, the noise. There's a few sound effects. Then years later, when Oliver Stone did his movie on the doors, he cleverly started the movie with the scene of Jim Morrison in the studio recording that poetry that became American Prairie, and he used that particular cut because it was just a brilliant way to start the movie. The very first thing you hear in The Door's movie is my little synthesizer making little woo-woo noises.

Oliver Stone wanted to keep things as realistic as possible, and the original plan was to get the remaining doors, Robbie and John on their original old equipment as much as possible and go to Cherokee studios where they recorded and have the original engineer, Bruce Botnick, and the original producer, Paul Rothschild, there to make an aesthetic prerecord sound for the rehearsal scene in the rehearsal place in Venice Beach, where they did *Break on Through* and *Light My Fire.*

Unfortunately, I guess Ray and Oliver Stone weren't getting along so well, so Robbie called me and asked me if I would go pretend to be Ray pretending to be himself back in the rehearsal days and play keyboards on, I guess, I think it was *Light My Fire* and *Break on Through*.

I did that. I'm in the movie in two places. hen you hear the keyboards, if you watch the movie, the keyboards in those rehearsal scenes is actually me playing them.

Tony: I've got it on Blu-ray. Now when I pop it in, it's going to make a big difference there. You actually put a band together with Robbie, I guess, and did a tour?

Arthur Barrow: Yes, we've had a band for the last few years, and about three years ago, we completed an album, mostly with stuff that Robbie and I had written and that we recorded here at my studio, and had an opportunity to play in New York City. I guess it was like three or four years ago, maybe. We did that, and we've been doing gigs on and off. We were in a little East Coast tour a year ago in December, and then a couple of gigs in between, and then we did about a month-long tour in August, where we went for every place from the South Dakota, where they have the annual biker rally. Which was a pretty much of a trip. The most entertaining part about that is even though it had rained, and it was an outdoor thing, and the field was all muddy, still we had a pretty good audience, a couple of thousand people out there.

A lot of them were sitting there on their bikes with their loud pipes, and we'd play a song, and they'd fire up their motorcycles and rev them up! This enormous sound would come from all these pipes. That was part of their applause.

Tony: How cool.

Arthur Barrow: If they liked the song, the louder they'd rev up their motors. We went from there too, and we also hit Chicago and Detroit, and played at the Cutting Room in New York City, and a couple other places on the East Coast, and ended up in Florida, and finally back here.

Then we had another little string of gigs just recently. Last week was, or I guess the week before last was, apparently it's the 50th anniversary of the opening of the Whiskey A Go-Go Club. It's been open for 50 years, and so they had about a week long of various bands playing to celebrate that, and I guess we were the first band. They invited Robbie, since the Doors were such a big attraction at the Whiskey back in the day. We played that, and then another place called the Canyon Club, and even played Las Vegas, which was quite an experience. Then we played the NAMM show.

Tony: Right, sure, of course.

Arthur Barrow: Yes, the Big National Association of Music Manufacturers, a big music biz thing with thousands of people, and we had a nice billing on Saturday night after the show on the big main stage in between the Marriott and the Hilton there.

Tony: What's the name of the group?

Arthur Barrow: We're calling it *Robbie Krieger's Jam Kitchen*.

Tony: Jam Kitchen?

Arthur Barrow: Yes, sort of as a, based on Soul Kitchen.

Tony: Sure, right, yes.

Arthur Barrow: Maybe trying to, hopefully we'll get in on the jam band circuit or something.

Tony: Right.

Arthur Barrow: We play a lot of instrumental originals, and then also, of course, we play a few Doors songs too. We even play a couple of Zappa songs. We've been opening with *Chunga's Revenge*. I've been playing *Cosmic Debris*. I get to sing it, so that's fun.

Tony: How great to play with those guys who are legends.

Arthur Barrow: It is cool and, it's a great honor, but it is sort of just also what I do. Honestly, a lot of times, I'm sure it sounds a lot better from the outside than it actually is experiencing it on the inside. For example, Las Vegas was a disaster.

Tony: Really?

Arthur Barrow: Yes, we got there, we had this long sound check at 5 pm and everything was just wrong with the PA and just problems and loud crashing noises coming out. Finally, get done with that at 7 and then we're supposed to go on at 11 because there's two opening acts and go back to the hotel to rest a little bit and then we find out, well, it's not going to be till 11.30… and then we find out it's not going to be till 12 that we start.

I'm getting old. I'm almost 62. Started at midnight, really? We get up there and there's still massive equipment problems so bad that we even have to just stop the show altogether. I'm standing up there really trying to fix something. I'm looking at my watch, it's 12.15 and we haven't even really gotten underway yet.

It was just massive equipment problems. Then there was this huge low-end feedback and then there was inadequate power or something so my bass amp kept cutting out and then it would make this horrible feedback sound and, my God, it was just a nightmare!

Tony: Was it your equipment or the venue's equipment?

Arthur Barrow: I think, I got the amp home and it now seems to be working just fine. I think that our road manager said there was some issue with power fluctuation that they were inadequately just juiced and I don't know what happened. It was just insane.

Tony: It just happened.

Arthur Barrow: The only good news is that in Las Vegas the martinis are only six bucks so I had a nice martini at three o'clock in the morning! AND they still allow smoking in those places, in the club and in the casinos. I shouldn't be on the radio dissing the entire city of Las Vegas. No. It's a wonderful place.

Tony: No, I love the place.

Arthur Barrow: I'm not a gambler. No, they don't get my money that way.

Tony: So how did you get into the Zappa band?

Arthur Barrow: Don Preston had given me Frank's home phone number at some point along the line. Don and I had a band there for a while with Bruce Fowler called *Loose Connection* and I kept meeting more and more people connected with Zappa. I even knew a guy who, before I got in the band, invited me to go down to the record plant where Frank was working on the *Zoot Allures* album.

I saw him recording drums for, I think it was *Wind up working at a gas station*. It was either that or *Disco Boy*. I can't remember now. Anyway, so I briefly met him then. A friend of mine called me up and said he just heard that Zappa was firing Terry and Patrick and was looking for a new drummer and bass player. I figured, well, this is my chance to dial this number.

I called him up and got him on the phone. I told him that I'd learned that melody at *Inca Roads* off the record by ear and played it as a bass exercise. I think that perhaps he didn't quite believe me, so he asked me if I knew the middle section of *St. Alfonso*. I said "Yes, sure, I'm familiar with it." He says "Well, transcribe that off the record and play that for me at your audition here."

I think maybe he said "Call me back next week and I'll tell you when and where." I got the record and put it on my reel-to-reel tape recorder and slowed it down from 7 1/2 to 3 3/4 to make it easier to figure out all those fast, funny little notes that I did. I went into my audition and I got there early and got to know the crew a little bit and plugged into a bass amp. He got in and I introduced myself. I said "Well, here's that thing that you asked me to learn." I whipped it out and he says "Well, I hear a few wrong notes in there, but you have potential."

I understand that he heard about 30 bass players the day before I was there, and probably 25 or 30 when I was there. It's like a cattle call. The word gets out and everybody in the world wants to come audition.

I played a few times and then he said "Okay, well, I'm going to hire you on a sort of a tentative basis and see how it works out. I'll let you know at the end of the week or something if you have the job or not."

Then I think it was the next day he brought in a bunch of music to sight read. Although I was never the greatest sight reader in the world, I could read his stuff pretty well because I just understood a little bit about the way he thought musically. If I saw something that was a bar of 5/8 or 5/16 or a quintuplet, it's almost inevitably going to go one, two, one, two, three. If it's a seven, it's going to go one, two, one, two, one, two, three.

Whereas the other guys who I'm sure were better readers, but if they'd come across a quintuplet or something like that, they'd choke and they'd say "What the hell is that?" I would just breeze right through that stuff because I was familiar with it.

Frank thought I was pretty good and we took a break after that and took me aside and said "You don't have to wait till the end of the week. You're hired now. You're one of the best bass players I ever played with." I just about jumped 30 feet in the air, it felt like. That's how I got in the band.

Yes, it was like the summer of '78, August. I think, it was June or July when we did the auditions, but that summer. Vinnie Colaiuta joined that band at the same time as me. Now there's a guy who knows all the odd time signatures.

Tony: Right! Hopefully the drummer knows what he's doing.

Arthur Barrow: I can feel them all the way up to 11, but when it goes to 11, I can't really feel it.

Tony: You were actually being the band leader in rehearsals before Frank came in and took over.

Arthur Barrow: Right, the *CloneMeister* was the position.

Tony: Is that a real word, or did you guys make that up? The *CloneMeister*?

Arthur Barrow: No, it's a word Frank made up. One of my jobs would be to pick a song I wanted to do, and I would sit down with a record and transcribe it and write down all the parts and then clone it, so to speak, and then teach it to the band.

Tony: Right.

Arthur Barrow: I can't say I was the musical director or band leader or anything like that. A more apt analogy would be like drill sergeant, to tell you the truth. Starting with the second half of each rehearsal, rehearsals were about eight hours a day. Five days a week. When Frank would come in for the second half, he would, say "You do this and you do this, you arrange it and try different things/" and I'd be tape recorder, and we'd all be taking notes, and he'd put this here, put that there, and so on.

Then I'd go home at night and sit down with my notes in the tape recorder and make more notes as to who was supposed to do what when and how it went and all that stuff, and then I'd come in the next day for the first half of the rehearsal before Frank was there, and we'd go over the stuff we'd done the night before, and, of course, people would forget a lot of the stuff they were supposed to do, and I'd say "No."

I remember you were supposed to do that, and he'd go "Yes, okay." so we'd just run through it and drill it a few times until the band was playing it the way he'd tell us to play it the night before, and then he'd get in again, and then he'd, half the time he'd change it all up again!

Tony: Where did you guys practice?

Arthur Barrow: It was often at a sound stage, like a movie sound stage. It was Culver City Studios, which was, I think, part of the old MGM studios, so I don't know if you ever seen a sound stage, but it's a huge room, high ceiling, and he used those because he could set up his whole PA and lights system.

It was usually in one of those, or we did it in a few different ones around town. Some of the early rehearsals in '80 were at his warehouse, where he just set up an area with a stage, or a riser, not really a whole stage, but just a riser, and sort of we could set up the way we were set up on stage. We rehearsed there, but it would always end up in a sound stage before we left.

Tony: Now I understand that he used to record just everything. Was that the case when you were with him?

Arthur Barrow: When I was first in the band, he wasn't, except for just cassettes off the board mix, the front house board mix, he was not recording multi-track or anything, I don't think, most of the time at first, although he had a little two-track recorder that they record every night, but only his guitar tracks, only his guitar solos.

Tony: To use them later, probably.

Arthur Barrow: Yes, exactly, that's what he used on Joe's Garage when he'd fly guitar tracks in from other songs. Yes, later, by the time of the last tour, they were recording stuff, more multi-track, at least eight-track, maybe some of a 24-track. Then after I left the band, I know they had the whole recording truck with the 24-tracks and stuff.

Tony: What makes somebody get out of the band?

Arthur Barrow: There's certainly plenty of ex-Zappa musicians floating around. It can mean various things. In my case, I did it for two and a half years and I I'd seen people leave the band on poor terms with Frank, not getting along and, stayed in long enough to where they hated him or something.

I certainly didn't want that to happen. There were personal reasons for me. I also wanted to try to move on to the next phase of my life. I wasn't really that great of a road person. I just decided that the time had come and Frank asked me to do the next tour and I just explained I wasn't going to do it

Every time he put together a band after that though, he asked me if I wanted to do it. In fact, initially, I think it was January of '81, when he wanted to do a tour and then Vinnie pulled out too, so I think he realized he didn't have a band and so canceled plans for that tour until later in the year, but he still kept calling me to come up to the house to record things.

I was on *The Man From Utopia* and some of that stuff from that period and I would notice that he'd call me up and hire me for a lot of sessions and that was always fun because, those recording sessions paid pretty well and it was always cool to be up at Frank's house recording.

He'd have me up there for a few days and sort of butter me up and then say "You sure you don't want to change your mind and join the band?" I think the last '88 tour he asked me if I wanted to come be the second keyboard player or something like that. I think maybe he sensed that the trouble was brewing with relations in the band and that it would be handy if I were there to change positions if need be.

By the time the mid-'80s came, by '83, I worked with all those other people you mentioned, from Irene Cara to Billy Idol and just tons of people in there. It was a madhouse for about three, four years in there.

It was cool, a lot of fun. I got to, among other things, I got to play on a number one Academy Award winning song, *Take My Breath Away*. That's me playing basically all the instruments on there including samples of my voice but, of course, I got no credit for it. The album and everything says T*ake My Breath Away* by Berlin. That's sort of typical for album soundtracks. Musicians don't really get credit usually.

Tony: Yes, it's not like the movies where they have five million credits and you're bound to be in there somewhere.

Arthur Barrow: I do have an actual film credit in Scarface. They needed some lyrics written for some of the source music coming out of the disco jukebox or whatever in the nightclub scenes. I actually do have some film credit at the end of that, "Lyrics by Arthur Barrow." I get a few pennies now and then when that's shown on TV.

Tony: You go out to stand by the mailbox and wait for the mailman!

Arthur Barrow: It doesn't amount to a whole lot, but I certainly don't get any checks for anything related to Frank Zappa, that's for sure. Sometimes people say, they're surprised when they find that I don't! "You mean you're on the album but you don't get any residuals? You don't get any royalties from that?" The answer would be no, not that I ever expected them or was anything ever promised to me.

If you're a side man, you do sessions, you get paid for the session and that's it. Nothing else was offered or expected in that case, but just for the record, in case people think that I get rich every time a copy of Joe's Garage is sold, it's not the case.

There was a lot more that I benefited from that, other than compensation, that's for sure. I was very lucky to do it and I feel sorry for young people today who don't have that opportunity to get to play with somebody like Zappa. It just doesn't exist anymore as far as I can tell. I was one of the lucky few that was able to have the privilege of doing that.

Cal Schenkel

Cal Schenkel was an American artist known primarily for his iconic album cover artwork, particularly for his extensive collaboration with Frank Zappa and his band, The Mothers of Invention. Schenkel's surreal and often grotesque visual style became closely associated with Zappa's music during the late 1960s and throughout the 1970s.

Schenkel's work with Zappa includes designing album covers for many of Zappa's albums, such as "We're Only in It for the Money," "Uncle Meat," "Burnt Weeny Sandwich," and "Over-Nite Sensation." His distinctive art style, characterized by collage, surrealism, and dark humor, perfectly complemented Zappa's avant-garde musical aesthetic.

In addition to his collaboration with Zappa, Schenkel has worked with other artists and bands, creating album covers, posters, and other visual artwork.

Tony: Hey Cal! Where are you at today?

Cal Schenkel: I'm in Pennsylvania, in southeastern Pennsylvania, outside of Philly. Actually, I just got our electricity back about an hour ago. I'm sitting by the heater!

Tony: So how did you first meet up with Frank Zappa?

Cal Schenkel: Actually. when I got out of high school, which was in '64, I decided to take a year off before attending college. I was going to go to art school. I wanted to do a little traveling and to work a bit and before I settled down in the school.

A friend of mine and I hitchhiked to California, which is something that we had wanted to do at that time. It was the beginning of '65, before going to school. We hitchhiked to California and bummed around, lived on the beach in Venice for a while and hung out in Hollywood. My friend's a musician, so we went to clubs a lot. That was when I first discovered Frank, and I discovered the Mothers.

They didn't have any albums out yet. It was pre-*Freak Out*. Just hanging out in Hollywood, I saw Frank now and then a few times. I saw them perform in Hollywood. One night, I'm hitchhiking with some friends to go back to where we were staying. I think it was in Hermosa Beach. This car full of chicks picks me up and says "Hey, we're going to a session. Do you want to come along?" This is about two in the morning. I said to myself "Well, who's not going to come along with a car full of chicks?"

I had no idea what I was getting into! I wound up at one of the *Freak Out* recording sessions where Frank had put the call out to just bring in the crazy freaks wandering around Hollywood to make noise behind *Son of Monster Magnet* or one of the long crazy cuts. That was my informal introduction of Frank.

Then, like about a half a year later, maybe a little less, I'm back in Philly, and *Freak Out* had just come out. I picked up Dan and said, hey, that's that Zappa guy. I've got to get to this. I love it. This has got to be great.

My girlfriend at the time was a girl named Essra Mohawk. I had met her in art school.

Tony: She lives here in Nashville now.

Cal Schenkel: Yes, she lives in Nashville and performs. We played the *Freak Out* album a lot. She loved it. We both loved it. Then one night we see that the Mothers are performing in New York. I couldn't get away. I had classes or something. Sandy went up with my friends. The next thing she's up on stage with Frank and singing. He asked her to join the band. Miracle. She went to New York and joined the band for the summer when they came back to New York to play the Garrick Theater for this long, extended gig they did that summer. During that time, shortly after they met, she – well, Frank had done most of the art, the design and art for his first two albums.

Absolutely Free was just about to come out. He was really so busy with the Garrick show that he was looking for some help. Sandy suggested I meet him. I brought my portfolio up, showed it to him, and he offered me a job. I quit school, and that was that.

The first thing I did was a poster for the Garrick show, which was just basically spray paint saying pigs in the window. Then I did the light show with some melded slides and crazy stuff. Then we started working on some ads for *Absolutely Free*, which had just come out. The first big project was they were only for the money.

Tony: I heard that on that design, there were some of the celebrities that you had up there. You had to remove them, or did they take them out later?

Cal Schenkel: No, not actually, but it's convoluted, too, because, obviously because it's a satire of *Sgt. Pepper,* at least the basic premise and the design. There were ideas of a lot of people that he wanted to get in the shot that just couldn't show up. Now, Hendrix was there for the session, because Jimmy was hanging out with Frank a bit then. We went to one show at a club when they were performing in New York, and I think he came to the Garrick a few times and came over to the house a few times.

Right around that time when we were doing the shot, Frank invited him to come along. He is actually in the shot, but Frank had ideas for a number of people that couldn't make it, and so we had to do a giant collage of everybody else.

Tony: Was this in New York, or was this in LA?

Cal Schenkel: Yes, this was in New York. We were still living in New York. When MGM got the art, their legal department insisted that we don't actually do it the way we wanted to, and so Frank came up with the idea of just putting bars over everybody's eyes. They wanted to get releases from everybody, and half of the people in there were either somebody out of Frank's yearbook or some obscure photo I picked up somewhere. We just put bars over their eyes, and then at the last minute, they also insisted that we turn the package inside out. As far as I know, there was no actual real threat from the Beatles. It was simply MGM's legal department chickening out.

Tony: Tell me about herb Cohen.

Cal Schenkel: Frank had been with Herb since *Freak Out*, and I think actually Herb got the gig at the Garrick because he was good friends with Howard. I can't think of the guy's last name. He owned the Go-Go, Cafe Go-Go, where just about everybody played in the village, and the Garrick was free, so it was a good place for Frank to really develop his show.

Then we went to Europe with that show, and then when we came back, I think at that time, and the Garrick run was over. This was the winter of '67. Yes, and so Frank wanted to move back to L.A., and I was ready to get out of there too.

So we set up shop in L.A., and Frank had been wanting to start his own record company, so they put together two separate record companies, I guess, for various legal reasons, Bizarre and Straight.

I was pretty much the Bizarre art department totally, and then since there was just really too much work for one person, John Williams came in and handled Straight. Herb, I guess, had the rights and worked with Frank on the Lenny Bruce stuff, and actually Frank was going to use some of that in a mix for that album that actually became *We're Only for the Money*.

I think really what happened was because *Sgt. Pepper* was such a phenomenon, he really changed around a lot of what he wanted to do with it, and of course everything was constantly in flux with his albums. He'd start out something and then it would turn into something else, and then it would turn into two albums, and then part of it would become *Reuben and the Jets*, and that would be something else.

Because he was so involved with every aspect, he didn't really have to deliver something to somebody else's specifications, and it was a complete package of everything.

Trout Mask became about because Frank and Don were friends from high school in Lancaster, California. I had this little art studio there that I worked out of and did *Trout Mask* and *Uncle Meat* and a Wild Man Fisher cover.

I worked on GTOs and then John Williams took over. I started on *Alice Cooper,* Alice Cooper's first album that Frank produced. Alice had come in with a painting for the cover. There really wasn't a lot to do on that anyway.

That was a big mushroom ballooning of everything happening that year, '68, '69.

I'll tell you a little bit about the log cabin too. Which was another really amazing period. It only lasted a couple of months when we first moved back to California. I was up at Frank's place up on the top of Laurel Canyon, Woodrow Wilson area. I didn't have my car. I had to go down to the studio and Janet, who is in *200 Motels* was Moon's governess. She had an old Jaguar that actually had belonged to Captain Beefheart, but was a really funky old Jaguar. That was the only car available. I took the Jag and I drove down to the corner of Mulholland and Laurel Canyon Boulevard. I'm waiting there at the light to turn left onto Laurel Canyon. Gail's sister was with me too, as I recall. I know this actually happened. It wasn't just a dream.

I'm waiting at the corner and I notice there's these two young kids hitchhiking, a long-haired guy and a girl. The next thing I know, they're getting in the back of the car. I thought, well, they must have thought I'd motioned them to get in!

I turn left, I go down Laurel Canyon, and I ask them where they're going. I'm just going down the bottom of the hill and didn't get a response at all, just nothing. I get to the bottom of the hill and said, well, I'm just going a little further. I'm just going down the Melrose. I don't know where you want to get out… but nothing. I get to the studio, I park, and I tell them "Well, this is it. This is where I'm going, so I'm not going any further." They just sit there.

I go up to my studio. They're still in the back of the car. I look out about 10 minutes later, they're still in the car. A short time later I look out and they're gone. No words spoken at all at any time! Well, I don't know, maybe they were on acid or something or whatever. Then I look out and about 15 minutes later I look out and they're back in the car.

They had gone to the market next door and got some loaf of bread and some lunch meat and they made sandwiches and they're sitting in the back of the car having their lunch.

This went on for a while and every once in a while I look out and they're still there. The next thing I finally look out and they're gone. That's the story. The crazy hitchhiker. I got a kick out of it, yes. I guess so. I wrote a song about it. That's worthy of a song.

Tony: So… Edward Beardsley, that's who designed it.

Cal Schenkel: Yes, Edward Beardsley, right, was the artist.

Tony: You did the 200 motels animation sequence, didn't you?

Cal Schenkel: I worked on that. Yes, I designed it. I did the production design. I worked with an art director in London. I did most of the set designs. The whole thing was such an amazing event. They filmed it in like five days on video. It was one of the first video productions.

Then there were some issues with a piece of it It was integral with the filming. Frank decided that we would animate it instead, because the video, the image part of the video was no good. The soundtrack was good. We used the soundtrack and turned that into, the crazy Mark and Howard bit. I think it took about two months to put together.

Tony: Yes, well, that's a lot of money to spend just for going, I think we'll animate this. you just spent a lot of money there, really. I guess I would take advantage of that, too, if I knew I had an animation department.

Cal Schenkel: Yes, it was really a lucky break, actually, that the video was no good, because that, to me, went awry.

Tony: Now, you've got, you're still running the RALF.com, your site for your own artwork.

Cal Schenkel: Yes. R-A-L-F.

Tony: I'm looking at it right now. It's got all kinds of stuff.

Cal Schenkel: Yes, I have some prints, and I usually have some hand-done stuff, and whatever I'm working on that's affordable, I put up. I'm in the midst of redoing it all, which is constant anyway.

Tony: Sure.

Cal Schenkel: I have a bunch of new projects that I hope to have up within the next month.

Tony: People getting them signed wouldn't be a problem?

Cal Schenkel: No, everything is always signed, anything that I do. Everything I sell is either hand-done or I do have prints, I hand-print them myself, and they're hand-signed. I occasionally do a limited edition and, other affordable art, but I also do less affordable art.

Most of that I do either on commission or, in conjunction with a show. I had a show in Chicago last summer, and I'm working on some new work, larger pieces for an event coming up. I don't have anything quite scheduled yet, but I hope to be doing more traveling shows, too.

Occasionally I'll do like a record store event with a variety of stuff and, of course, I always sign albums, too, when I do stuff like that. I'm sure I'll make it to Nashville one of these days near you!

Tony: Now, have you done work with other bands?

Cal Schenkel: I haven't done a lot of records or CD work before.

Tony: Isn't it terrible that the albums kind of went away? Now you have an MP3. and there's no artwork at all.

Cal Schenkel: Right. That's the thing. I think it would really help with sales to do productions that actually do the art as part of the whole deal, like it used to be.

Tony: Albums are coming back.

Cal Schenkel: Yes. They're making their way back. That's one reason probably, too, for the packaging… as well as the vinyl quality. Most of the CD stuff I've done besides for Frank has been either smaller bands, local bands, people I know, or people that contact me, and I'll do a little production.

I did Tom Waits' first three covers. I was never really that much into getting involved with the music as much as that I really enjoy working for Frank because I could really be creative. Lately I've got some interesting things happening. There's a beer company in California. They actually did a series of beers with labels from Frank's early albums as the label, the beer label. He wants me to do a series of posters for his company, so I may be pursuing those. He's expanding, too. They just opened in Chicago, so you'll probably hear more about them. It's very popular in California.

Tony: Now, as we speak, I'm holding a *Brisk. T*hey make lemonade, and they make cool, weird bottle covers by different artists. I'll send you their contact information.

Cal Schenkel: Yes, that'd be neat. I'd be real interested in that.

Tony: This one's strange, which is good. They're not trying to stick to a certain look or whatever. They're just going with what's cool.

Cal Schenkel: That's good. They let the artist be creative, it sounds like. That's why the company I work with... because they're real, very interesting.

Tony: Now, if people want to keep in contact with you or see what's going on, is Facebook good for you, or what's a good way?

Cal Schenkel: Yes, I do Facebook. I have a lot of friends all over the world, and I do Facebook. I have a mailing list too There's a form on my website.

Tony: Which is RALF.com.

Cal Schenkel: Yes, that's the best way. I think it was '94 when I got my website. It was early, because I managed to get a four-letter website. It was, after a couple years, it was hard to find anything with the combination that we've worked. Yes, so that's the best way to reach me. Yes, all kinds of stuff online.

Tony: I'm actually looking through my collection of records here. I've got *Lumpy Gravy, Uncle Meat, Hot Rats, Burt Weenie Sandwich...* the list is so long here! You did T*inseltown Rebellion*, didn't you? I always loved that cover.

Cal Schenkel: Yes, that's one that was fun. I liked doing that collage. Now, that was a lot of work back then! It was all done by hand. With photos, Real cut and paste. Then having to try and match everything and get the printer to do it right. whereas now I can do all that myself and just send them a file, which is nice.

I like Photoshop and a few other image programs. I work on a PC. I started on a PC because it was much more affordable, and my cousin was a network guy, so he managed to get me a really nice machine. It went back in the '90s, when they were more expensive. I started on PC, and, of course, before long, you could do anything on PC.

Tony: Mac too?

Cal Schenkel: Yes, I like them both, but I started on the PC, but the programs are pretty much the same. Now I use a tablet, and I have a Chromebook, too, that I use for online stuff.

CANDY ZAPPA

Candy Zappa is the sister of the iconic musician Frank Zappa. While not as prominently involved in the music industry as her brother, Candy has made occasional appearances in Frank Zappa's work and has been involved in various projects related to his legacy.

Candy Zappa contributed background vocals to some of her brother's recordings, including the albums "Chunga's Revenge" (1970) and "You Are What You Is" (1981). Additionally, she appeared in the film "200 Motels" (1971), a surrealistic musical film directed by Frank Zappa and Tony Palmer.

Beyond her involvement in Frank Zappa's projects, Candy Zappa has also been active in preserving her brother's legacy. She has participated in interviews, documentaries, and events commemorating Frank Zappa's life and work. While not as well-known as her brother, Candy Zappa remains a recognizable figure among fans of Frank Zappa's music and his cultural impact.

Tony: How are you doing today?

Candy Zappa: Very well. Lovely day.

Tony: It's good that I could talk with you here. I know you've done interviews, and you've got a couple of books out, and your CD and things like that. I'm going to talk a little bit about those just because I've got you and I'm interested in all of it.

You're Frank's sister. I think everyone would know that! Just in case they go "Hey, she has the same last name as Frank!"

Candy Zappa: I've encountered people that look at the name and they don't connect.

Tony: Right.

Candy Zappa: Then all of a sudden they'll go "Are you related?" I go "Well, yes, I'm his sister." Then they have coronaries and whatever! They can't believe it!

Tony: Right.

Candy Zappa: Okay. Yes. Okay.

Tony: Now, you guys all grew up out in the Palmdale area of California. I've been out there quite a few times. I like the place. Do you ever make it out there much anymore or you stay more in the city?

Candy Zappa: We grew up in, well, we didn't grow up, but we lived in Lancaster for about a year and a half. Yes, I have a lot of friends that are still out there. We go out there. Nolan and I go out there all the time, to have dinner with friends and just visit with our people and have a good time.

Tony: Are you the youngest of all the brothers and sisters?

Candy Zappa: Yes, I am the last of the last. My father was married once before my mom. He had a daughter named Anne and she is my sister. She's 20 years older. There's actually five siblings.

Tony: Frank started being a full time musician and recording and all kinds of stuff. How old were you at that point when he was just starting out?

Candy Zappa: When everything started happening, I was about 14 or 15 years old. He when he did the *Freak Out* album in '66, I was like, well, let's see, 15. Right. Yes. It was quite an exciting time because he would come over to the house and regale us with tales of who he met and people that he worked with and, just everything.

It was just cool to listen to him. He'd come over and he'd show me songs that he'd written. I was supposed to sing, I don't know if the on the *Absolutely Free* album, *Status Back Baby*. That was I was supposed to sing that. He was teaching it to me and everything. Something happened. I don't know what or why nothing came of it.

Also in '69, I think he was going to put an album of songs and have me sing them. The album was going to be called *My Brother is a Mother*. Then my husband that I was married to at the time, didn't want me to do it. Frank said "Well, I don't want to step on any toes." That got killed, too. That's where the title of my book came from. Since, he was passed. It was *My Brother was a Mother.*

Tony: When the first album, *Freak Out* was really unique. I think nobody had ever done anything like that. It wasn't your typical '60s album for sure. What did you guys think when you heard it? Were you thinking "Who's going to buy this" or "This is so advanced people won't understand it." What was your thought on it?

Candy Zappa: When he when Frank came over to the house, the day he brought the album over, he was wearing the fur coat that he wore on the cover of the album. My mom was doing mom things. She was changing the sheets on the bed. We had this cheesy little record player. We're in the room where mom was working and he puts the album on and we're listening to *Hungry Freaks Daddy*, which I thought was really cool.

Then it came to *Who are the Brain Police?* The part where it goes "I think I'm going to die." I looked at mom. She looked at me and Frank was just enthralled. He says "Isn't this great?" I said "Yes, Frank, it's bitchin'!". We were taken aback. Still, I was there. I was listening to it and I learned everything. I know all the lyrics. Yes, it was a good album.

Tony: I don't know how it did actually in the '60s when it came out. I've never looked into, record sales or things like that. Do about how many copies they moved at that time? I know it sells, over time, the numbers really add up. Was it a relatively big at that time or what?

Candy Zappa: I think *Freak Out* sold pretty well for having no airplay whatsoever. I think it sold a million copies, something to that effect. My figures could be wrong. I don't know. There's other people that know more about this than I do. I think it went from word of mouth because I have a lot of people on Facebook that write to me and say, "I was introduced to your brother's music by somebody else who said, you've got to sit down and listen to this."

People were showing each other Frank's music and everybody was just blown away. You have to remember, the '60s was the hippie time. They would all get stoned and listen to this stuff and they thought it was magic. they're like on LSD listening to the one about wandering around barefoot and I *will love everyone, I will love the police as they kick the shit out of me on the street.*

They would hear that and they're going "yes, this is great. I can dig this." One time Frank was playing at some theater. My dad, mom, and me and my brother Carl were there to attend. Here we are. dressed up in our Sunday go-to-meeting clothes, and here are all these hippie dudes and girls outside with their feathers and bells and barefoot and leather and whatever. They're just checking us out like, oh my God. If they knew who we were.

Tony: Right. Exactly.

Candy Zappa: We got to see the show and it was an experience.

Tony: Now when Frank did that record, was he living at the house with you guys?

Candy Zappa: No, he was already out of the house by then.

Tony: Did he change what he was able to do? After becoming famous? I would assume after he came out with a successful album, he had a change in lifestyle, the way he lived, or things like that?

Candy Zappa: Yes. He'd already been married once and split up from his first wife. He met Gail and they got together in '68. They were living in the house on Lookout Mountain Road in Laurel Canyon. It was like a free for all.

There was so many people there. There was a lot of people in the house. Another book was written about it by the lady that Frank used as his secretary, *Freak Out, My Life with Frank Zappa* by Pauline Butcher. She describes it in great detail about how many people were there, what was going on. It's a pretty definitive book about his lifestyle.

Then they moved to Woodrow Wilson Drive further up from Mulholland. There was a lot of people there too. Then one day Frank just decided to clean house and he got rid of everybody and he was getting down to work. He was really working. He would change his hours. Some days he'd work all night and sleep all day and then reverse it. He'd work all day and then sleep all night. He needed that privacy to get to work and make the music that he made.

Tony: He had a studio in the house at that time. Do you remember if that was one of the first things that he did was actually get some sort of studio in the house? Because I know a lot of the records were recorded elsewhere. In the later years he recorded them all at home basically. Was he working towards that do you think in the early days?

Candy Zappa: I think from what I remember I was like maybe 17. This was back in '67, '68. We'd go up to visit and there was a studio down there. Yes, I think that's primarily what he wanted to do. I think he got tired of the record companies screwing him over. He decided to just make his own company. Barking Pumpkin. He got tired of being screwed around by the studios. He worked on having the studio in his home so he could have full control, full creativity. Everything was his.

Tony: I know that you put out a record. I assume that's still out for people to be able to get. What's the easiest way to get a copy of that?

Candy Zappa: Yes, it is. It's a compilation of a lot of things that I've done over the past few years, maybe 20 years. Anyway, go to www.crossfirepublications.com, all one word. Just go on there and you'll see everything that's available, my book, the CDs. I think they're on Amazon too.

Tony: Yes.

Candy Zappa: Nolan – my husband Nolan's stuff is on there too, Nolan Porter. Yes, his CDs and everything are on there too.

Tony: Now what does Nolan do? Tell me about him.

Candy Zappa: Nolan, he's very big in the Northern Soul Movement. He never met Frank but he actually was at Frank's house one time with his manager, who managed Steppenwolf.

Nolan was classically trained. Frank had Nolan sit down and listen to a lot of rhythm and blues stuff along with rock and roll. He put out two albums in the early '70s. When Frank broke up the original Mothers, Jimmy Carl Black, Lowell George and Roy Estrada went over to Lizard Records where Nolan was making his album. They all met. They all got together and they recorded on Nolan's album.

Yes, so he's been around for a while. He walked away from it I think in the '80s, He just didn't pursue it. Then when we got together in '99, everything just exploded and we started working together, singing together and doing shows.

Then one day in 2006, I was contacted by the people in Wales where they have a northern soul show where they were flying out a lot of the groups from the '50s and early '60s and soul groups and putting on this show out there.

His popularity just took off!. He's doing pretty good and as a matter of fact, we're doing a show. It's called *A Mess Around on February 16th at Viva Cantina*. I'm shamelessly plugging this but, anybody who's local can go see it. He'll be singing seven of his songs. Yes, and he's doing very well. We just did a gig in Arizona and the audience was incredible. It was a 55-plus community and these guys just loved the hell out of us and that was worthwhile.

Tony: Now, did you guys meet because of your connection with the musicians that you knew?

Candy Zappa: No, actually what happened was - I was at a restaurant bar that was having a karaoke contest and this lady that has become a very good friend of ours came up to me. We started talking. She told me about Nolan. She told Nolan about me!. She'd known him for some time before she met me.

I guess one day – it wasn't happening fast enough. We weren't getting to meet each other fast enough. I think it was the day after his birthday in May of '99. She calls me up and says "Come on out to Leon's and let's have a drink and do some singing."

Nolan was there and I wasn't too thrilled. I figured I was just going to be sitting with the girls! There was Nolan looking at me and I saw his eyes and I went, God, this guy's already spent. He sprung. He already likes me.

Tony: Nice.

Candy Zappa: We sang that night together for the first time. We did *Too Much, Too Little, Too Late* by Denise Williams and Johnny Mathis. We're looking at each other going, wow, that's pretty good. Because we were harmonizing really nice. That just did it. We were hooked. We've been singing and we've been together ever since. Then we got married in 2007. This will be our 15th year together and our 7th year anniversary this year.

Tony: Have you recorded anything with him?

Candy Zappa: We did. We worked with a guy named Brian Hudson and he did some really interesting political songs. I think we're going to re-release some of them. They were very good. He's been working on re-releasing his album. I think I'll probably be doing some recording on that too. Yes. We've worked together. We've recorded together. We've done shows together. We've done a lot together.

Tony: That sounds great. Do you have any contact with any of the kids like Moon or Dweezil or anybody? How much do you have contact with all the family?

Candy Zappa: None really. I did see Dweezil in concert a couple of years back

Tony: When you're playing, do you stay local? Do you do festivals or things that are more around the country?

Candy Zappa: We just did a gig in Arizona. We were in Canada the year before last to do a prostate cancer fundraiser in honor of Frank. Let's see, Nolan's going to England and then Spain in July. I will be here. We did a New Year's Eve thing in Lancaster. it's all of a sudden somebody will call us up and say "Hey, we've got something happening, would you be interested?"

Tony: You're on Facebook too, so that's an easy way for people to keep up with you. By thee way, here did you get the name *Candy* from? Is that an old family name that they called you?

Candy Zappa: My brother Carl, when I was born, he was, I guess, fascinated with, because there was three boys in the house and here comes this little blue-eyed red-haired girl because everybody else had black hair and brown eyes. I must have been a real freak. Anyway, he looked at me and said, she's so sweet. Let's call her Candy.

Tony: That was easy enough. That's an easy way to get it. You were named.

Candy Zappa: I was named.

Tony: That's really good! When you're doing recordings, you're going by Candy Zappa or what are you going by? If you put out an album today, who would you?

Candy Zappa: I usually put Patrice and then in parentheses Candy and then Zappa.

Tony: I just want people to be able to, find you if they're looking for you or buy products or, whatever. Anything that you think is important?

Candy Zappa: Yes, just go to the crossfirepublications.com. My book is there. *My Brother Was a Mother Take Two*. I'm very proud of that book because it's got pictures in there that no one else has of the family. I wanted to start it from the very beginning. A lot of people have. They've taken other pictures that have gone around and around and around. Stuff I have, nobody has. Nobody has.

ESSRA MOHAWK

Essra Mohawk, also known as Sandra Hurvitz, was an American singer-songwriter and musician known for her eclectic style blending elements of rock, folk, jazz, and blues. She gained recognition in the 1960s and 1970s for her solo work as well as her collaborations with various artists and bands.

Mohawk began her career as a songwriter, penning songs for artists such as The Shangri-Las and The Turtles. She released her debut album, "Primordial Lovers," in 1969, which showcased her distinctive voice and songwriting style. Throughout the 1970s, Mohawk continued to release solo albums, including "Essra Mohawk" (1974) and "E-Turn" (1976), which further established her as a unique talent in the music industry.

In addition to her solo career, Mohawk has collaborated with numerous musicians over the years, including Jerry Garcia and Carole King.

Tony: How did you wind up originally meeting Frank? What happened there?

Essra Mohawk: I was walking down the street one day with a couple of friends from L.A. We were right across the street from the Garrick Theater. They were walking down Bleecker Street. I'd gone with them to New York. They were in from L.A. We met in Philly. They were friends of Cal Schenkel, and we'll talk more about Cal in a bit. He was the artist, graphic artist that did all the covers for Frank. I knew him from PCA, Philadelphia College of Art.

Now it was about a year later after that. These girls came to visit him, and I went with them to New York, and there on Bleecker Street, they saw Frank heading our way because he was heading towards the Garrick, I guess, to go play. They yelled out, Ben Franks. Cantors. These are hangouts in L.A. where I had never been because I, unlike them, was not from L.A.

He let us all in for free thinking we were all from L.A. until he got to know that I was actually. what he ended up calling "That strange little person from Philadelphia!"

Tony: Nice!

Essra Mohawk: Yes, we all somehow got to hang out with him after, and we all got to know each other, and he got... I'll let you ask another question. I'm stopping here.

Tony: So...

Essra Mohawk: That's how we met.

Tony: I know that now you performed with the mothers a few times, or what did you do with them?

Essra Mohawk: I played with them three times a night every night and also opened to them three times a night every night. I think some nights we were only two shows. Weekends were three. Then I played... He heard me play and asked me to join the band right away, so I played whenever they played. I was one of them. Yes. The first female mother.

Tony: Right. Exactly.

Essra Mohawk: I wish I had stayed longer. I was young and the wide world was calling me.

Tony: Of course.

Essra Mohawk: Come, see all this, come to California, come to here, come there. So I did.

Tony: Your first album... was that produced by Frank?

Essra Mohawk: No. It was going to be. We had a strange, unusual disagreement over Billy Mundi, great drummer. When we were recording the first song, the song that he performed with the mothers... one of my songs. That's actually the first one we were going to record because everybody knew it.

All of it was good except the drums were a little stiff and at the end Billy took off on his own, it was great, it really grew. I suggested, I said "Frank, couldn't Billy play like that, let the record groove from the top, instead of when it's over?

Tony: Right...

Essra Mohawk: He said "Who's producing this album anyway?" He didn't say it so like it was funny. It was just the way he said it made you want to open a hole in the floor and fall through.

Tony: Yes, I understand.

Essra Mohawk: Looking back on it now, I've written a book, or actually the book is being written, I've got a lot of stuff to add about The Mothers too, but there's a lot of stuff in there. One of the things I explain in the book is that now I know what I should have said when he said "Who's producing this album anyway?" I should have said "You are, that's why I'm asking you this question!"

Tony: Right, you're asking the producer.

Essra Mohawk: I was 19 years old, and, I just, we didn't really like authority figures back then.

Tony: No, of course not.

Essra Mohawk: I basically said "You're not!" and I walked out, and the project was continued with Ian Underwood, who totally mismanaged, didn't know what he was doing, he was young, he also was very young.

Tony: Now this was what, '67?

Essra Mohawk: Yes. '68, actually, when we recorded the album. '67 is when I joined the band.

Tony: I see, okay.

Essra Mohawk: I was in the band for a while before we started working on the album, before he even signed me as a solo artist. I was just a member of the band, and then he wanted to call me, he did, he called me Uncle Meat.

Tony: Cool!

Essra Mohawk: That was fine, as long as I was, as a character in The Mothers, it made sense. He wanted me to continue to use that name for my solo project… really? I said "No, no. no, I won't. I don't want to be Uncle Meat."

Finally he gave in on that point, and he said "Well, if you don't want to make money from the name, I will." I said something he always said. I said "More power to you."

Tony: Wow.

Essra Mohawk: That's what he did. He ended up calling something *Uncle Meat,* and it wouldn't have mattered what he called it. It was Frank Zappa. It was the name that sold his stuff was Frank Zappa.

Tony: Yes, right.

Essra Mohawk: As well it should, because he's just one Frank Zappa and there's a lot of copycats.

Tony: It's cool that you were involved with that at all. Not very many people in the world can say that.

Essra Mohawk: Yes, it was wonderful. I was thrilled to be in that band. That was a wonderful band. It just was the best combination of musicians.

That original band had something magical. Yes. I'd never heard anywhere before or since. Actually there was a glimmer of it accidentally. Frank's ghost came through the studio several years ago. Billy Mundi came through here with an artist he wanted to produce. We went and he played a song with me and we went to the studio where I had been working.

Sax player Jeff Coffin and some other guys were there tracking something. It wasn't our session. I was just showing the studio, All of a sudden, while me and Billy were sitting there like, on the couch in the control room, all of a sudden, it turned into *The Mothers.* What we were listening to was exactly the music that we made back then, all the way back then at the Garrick Theater in '67. Billy turned and looked at me. We both knew, we both heard it. When they stopped the machine, these guys, they had no idea what they had done and how lame it was.

Tony: Yes.

Essra Mohawk: They recorded over it and did something real, I hate to say it because the great players know, but it was really lame. They did something real ordinary.

Tony: Sure.

Essra Mohawk: Just like a horn line. Instead of this brilliant stuff that just blew out. I think it was Frank's spirit there because me and Billy were in the room. Me and Billy agreed that Frank just came through and gave us a taste of what was.

These people here and now, they couldn't appreciate the brilliance. They thought they were making a mistake.

Tony: Now, you've done a dozen albums. How many albums have you, how many have you done so far? About a dozen.

Essra Mohawk: I think that actually 11 of them are studio albums. 11 different studio albums. I'm going to do the 12th one. I hope to be getting on to that by fall. Because right now, I'm in the middle of reissuing Primordial Lovers again.

Finally, with the album cover that more exemplifies what I wanted to do, my original concept back then. I gave in on the point in life, you give in on things you shouldn't. You don't give in on things you should. You don't know until you're looking back and then it's 2020.

Tony: Right.

Essra Mohawk: I shouldn't have given in on this, on the cover. Because it would have been a beautiful, full-color cover representing heaven and earth superimposed on the two naked bodies. Instead, it was a black-and-white photo that you couldn't even tell they were bodies. I have to work with that because they didn't save any of the other photos.

Tony: Yes.

Essra Mohawk: That's me and Mrs. Mohawk on the floor there.

Tony: Is it really?

Essra Mohawk: Naked on the floor.

Tony: I think John and Yoko ripped you off there a little bit later on, didn't they? Who was first on that?

Essra Mohawk: I know it's like people look at it and go, is that like legs? As one friend put it was so subtle "It ain't right."

Tony: Right.

Essra Mohawk: I had one album on Reprise, which is Warner Brothers. The second, which is Primordial Lovers, which was originally released on Reprise, and the third one, which was initially released on Electro Asylum, that's the one that has the cover. The blue album.

Tony: I see. I see. You mentioned Cal Schenkel, and he mentioned you when I talked to him. I didn't know there was a you and Cal connection until he mentioned it.

Essra Mohawk: I got him the Zappa gig. We were college sweethearts. We were college sweethearts.

Then a year later, I had been in New York, he had been in L.A., I came back to Philly. He came back to Philly first, then I came back to Philly. Meanwhile, a year before that, I guess while Cal was in L.A., I went with another friend of mine from my neighborhood. We dropped acid and went to New York to see the Mother's. Opening for the Mothers was Satyrs. They opened for the Mothers a lot. He was a brilliant flute player. Jeremy Steig is the son of William Steig, the inventor of Shrek.

Now, I don't know what happened to Jeremy. I think he went down to South America or something. Anyway, he's a great player. I saw these two bands and they were both brilliant. I was on acid and a year later I ended up in both those bands.

I was just thinking, maybe I should drop acid and go see the Rolling Stones. A year later I could be there. It's true. That is true.

Getting back to Cal, so now I was in The Mothers and I was living with Frank. It was at 180 Thompson Street. Frank was doing everything himself… he did all the art. He said he needed an art department guy.

Tony: Where was this?

Essra Mohawk: That's New York. Yes. Okay. Still 1967.

Tony: Right.

Essra Mohawk: I'm going to zip around a little bit. Cal's who first introduced me to The Mothers, when he first came back from L.A. that time, he played me Freak Out.

Tony: Right.

Essra Mohawk: Wow, what a great band. Loved them. Then, of course, I went and heard them and loved that. Now I was in the band and Frank was saying he needed a guy for the art department. I said "I know just the guy." Because see, Cal's style was exactly right for Frank. They were two halves or two sides of the same coin. I always think it was like Cal was like a very, passive artist. Frank, a very aggressive band leader.

Tony: Right.

Essra Mohawk: They worked really well together all those years. I said "I know just the guy." He says "Well, let me see his stuff." I ran to Philly and I helped Cal put together a portfolio of stuff that I knew that Frank would love. I ran back to New York and showed the portfolio to Frank. He was wowed. "Go get him." he said. I went back. Got Cal, brought him to Frank. Made it happen!

Tony: Yes, and they worked together a lot. He did quite a few album covers.

Essra Mohawk: He did ten, I think... it was what, ten more years of album covers. Until Frank passed, I guess. Frank was around for a while. I don't know what happened. I know that even beyond Frank's death, Cal continued to do the reissues. Yes. It's a lifetime of work and well-earned renown for Cal. I'm proud to have made the match.

Tony: Yes, that is really great. Isn't that always the case? It's that one thing in everybody's life that changes everything. You think "I'm glad that happened or I wouldn't be where I am now."

So you've had songs recorded by Cindy Lauper, Tina Turner, and you've worked with John Mellencamp and Carole King.

Essra Mohawk: Shall I give you a John Mellencamp story? He used to call me all the time for advice. In fact, when I moved to LA, I met him in New York and did some background recordings. We got to be friends. He always called me for advice and he tracked me down. He called my mom, found out where I was and called me. When they wanted to change his name to Johnny Cougar, he asked my advice. I said "Well, John Mellencamp is a really strong name." I said "If you do change your name to Johnny Cougar, you're only going to end up changing it back to John Mellencamp."

He knew I always could tell him the truth and that's why he always came to me for advice. Because I could see the bigger picture and always would steer him the right way. When he came to LA and played and opened for someone that was more popular than him, I brought 8 or 10 people to The Whiskey to hear him, to be a little cheering section for him. He would take me backstage and introduce me with all kinds of respect to everybody.

Then he said, "Whichever one of us makes it first will help the other one." We agreed on that. Then I went to see him in Philly. I went to see him at whatever arena it was... Spectrum or something. I said "Boy, I can't wait!" I knew that he had tickets for us. I figured I'd see him backstage. I said "Wow, he's going to help me!"

Tony: Yes.

Essra Mohawk: He left us general admission tickets. I just pointed at the sky and it rained. We sold our tickets for $5 apiece.

Tony: You got $10 out of it. Hey, there you go. You can say "I got a great story out of this. It's all good material."

Essra Mohawk: Yes. It's all great material. All goes into the book.

Tony: Or maybe even write a number one song about it!

Essra Mohawk: Yes!

Tony: Hey, we've only got a few minutes left… let's talk about Frank Zappa. Maybe some things that were personal, or things that maybe somebody doesn't know.

Essra Mohawk: There's one story in my book about him and Eric Clapton. I got to open for The Cream and a lot of people. Like I'd be opening for The Mothers. I remember when The Cream first played their first time in New York, in the United States, I believe.

Eric was in awe of Frank, so they're in that little apartment, 180 Thompson, there's Eric sitting on the floor, looking up at Frank, sitting in a chair, they've got their guitars in their hands. I'm not going to tell this, so you've got to read the book.

Tony: What's a good way for people to get your book?

Essra Mohawk: Email the hell out of me and say, "Essra, finish the book! Essra, finish the book! Essra, finish the book!!"

The book, when it does come out, will be called *Tales of the Secret Diva,* and there's a lot of folks in there that you'll recognize and be interested to hear a different point of view than anyone's ever explained before.

I will say this about Frank that nobody might know, is that every day he woke up and he said "Another day, another dollar!"

Tony: I guess that sums it up... Another day, another dollar.

Essra Mohawk: I guess that was true, It's like he was the first yuppie. He was ahead of his time. He was like a man of the '80s, but with all the psychedelia of the '60s without any of the drugs.

Tony: Right.

Essra Mohawk: He was the ringmaster. He was the ringmaster. Everyone else enjoyed the show.

Tony: Yes. Isn't that something? That's a good way to put it. The amount of people that I've talked to that have played with him over the years, and all the things that have changed, of course, the style of music that he put out and all that. Just evolved with the time.

I'm still a big fan, of course, of the '60s group. That's probably my favorite of any of them. Because, like you say, it was the original one and there was really something there that was magic.

Essra Mohawk: It was that magic time. People really just expressed themselves in a way they haven't since. People seem to move away from that natural expression and everything is so contrived, especially here in Nashville, I might add. Very contrived.

Tony: Yes.

Essra Mohawk: Yes. Very disappointing. The results are all that matter, I guess. The means of getting there, isn't as important as what you get to.

Tony: The '60s were that really expressive time that you can't get away with nowadays. I wish it would come back, or at least a little bit of that feeling would come back.

Essra Mohawk: I maintained it, I feel, in my music and in my life. By the way, I'm going to be putting out a DVD. It's a UK company that's releasing a DVD compilation. It has all kinds of stuff from, all these decades. Don Preston's in there and Bunk Gardner's in there. Denny Wally, who's in the Magic Band. We're going to be working together. There's a lot of stuff up ahead.

Tony: They can keep up with you. *Essra Mohawk dot com.* Right?

Essra Mohawk: That's it. Go find me on Facebook. I'm a secret, yet I'm accessible.

Made in the USA
Columbia, SC
08 July 2024